What To Do? Christians and Ethics

What To Do? Christians and Ethics

Richard G. Jones

WIPF & STOCK · Eugene, Oregon

Wipf and Stock Publishers
199 W 8th Ave, Suite 3
Eugene, OR 97401

What to Do? Christians and Ethics
By Jones, Richard G.
Copyright©1999 Methodist Publishing - Epworth Press
ISBN 13: 978-1-5326-3062-0
Publication date 4/6/2017
Previously published by Epworth Press, 1999

Every effort has been made to trace the current copyright
owner of this publication but without success. If you have
any information or interest in the copyright, please contact the publishers.

Contents

General Introduction	vii
Introduction	ix

Part 1 The Project — 1

1. The Project Conceived — 3
2. Youth Fellowship — 8
3. The Businessman — 12
4. The Scientists — 16
5. The Mother — 20
6. The Long Arm of the Law — 24
7. A Résumé — 28
8. The Doctor — 32
9. The Lecturer — 36
10. The Minister — 40
11. Ethics in the Old Testament — 44
12. Ethics in the New Testament — 48
13. Sunday Lunch — 52

Part 2 Thinking Through the Issues — 59

14. Do Your Own Thing? — 61
15. How Not To Use the Bible — 67
16. The Bible – A Better Way — 73
17. Is Love Enough? — 79
18. Be Good, As a Rule — 85

Contents

19.	What Use Should the Church Be?	90
20.	How Special Is the Christian Way?	96
21.	Jesus and Compromise	101
22.	So Where Have We Got?	108
Further Reading		113

General Introduction

The great Swiss theologian, Hans Küng, has said that his aim in all his writings is to enable his readers to hold their faith with confidence and not with a bad conscience. This new series, prompted by the conviction that Christians need to think through their faith but often lack appropriate help in so doing, has a similar aim. Moreover, the assistance that it seeks to offer is related to another conviction: that many church members need persuading that theologians are concerned in any way with their problems and that theology can be at all relevant to their lives.

In such a situation, it is essential, we are sure, to begin with life and with church life. Only in that way can we be confident that we are dealing with grassroots issues. Plainly, however, it is not enough to identify the questions where they arise; we must also indicate the sources of help – if not of all the answers – in as non-technical a way as possible.

In some volumes, these tasks will be tackled in sequence; in others, they will be interwoven. Whatever the precise format, however, our hope is that, through this interaction, difficulties will be faced, fears dispelled, open discussion promoted, and faith informed and strengthened.

The books can either be read by individuals on their own or used in groups. We hope the questions at the end of each chapter will be useful both as a check that the text has been understood and as a spur to reflection and discussion.

Later volumes will deal with such issues as the existence of God, Jesus, the Holy Spirit, creation and providence, salvation, prayer, and presenting the gospel.

GRAHAM SLATER AND C. S. RODD

To Jack and Jasmine

Introduction

It is difficult to know quite how vast is one's debt when writing about Christian ethics. One is deeply grateful to one's parents and the close family of one's upbringing; to one's own family; and then to the church and the whole ethos conveyed in its worship and fellowship life; and then to the modern world, with its deep concern for what is right and good; and then to writers galore, to academics and theologians; and then to ordinary folk, one's neighbours and friends, constantly talking about the matters raised in this brief book. Behind all those agencies one cannot but believe that God is always trying to lure us towards the truth and the good, so one ends up profoundly thankful that this is not a barren world in which the puzzles of ethics, of what on earth we should do, remain in darkness and confusion.

Much gratitude too to the editors, who have patiently coaxed this study along, and to Derek Happs, who has done much typing with much patience.

RICHARD G. JONES

Part 1

The Project

1

The Project Conceived

Matthew, at seventeen, was thoroughly enjoying being in the sixth form and asking questions about everything without being slapped down as a nuisance. His RS teacher was especially responsive to his incessant exploration. 'Think it through for yourself,' he would say, after replying to the latest barrage of probing comment, 'but don't forget a and b and c, and for heaven's sake don't assume that all wisdom lodges in twentieth-century brains and that everyone before us was a simpleton.'

The Sunday night Youth Fellowship was also an especial pleasure because the leader had the same attitude and encouraged her group to test the cogency of everything they ever heard, in the church or anywhere else. She too drew attention to resources from the past, often remarking during a lively discussion, 'It's worth finding out what the great Christian thinkers have taught.'

In the Youth Fellowship the hottest debates were usually about moral issues. Abortion divided them deeply, and they had now agreed to keep off it. World debt came in for regular denunciation, as did nuclear power. The group tended, in fact, to have standardized opinions, but sometimes the discussions were very thoughtful. For example, one girl, in her first office job, asked what she should do when expected to answer the phone and often tell bare-faced lies. That evening, when Matthew went home, he kept his parents up late as he talked through all sides of the discussion and couldn't let it drop.

The next morning he had to sort out with his teacher what the topic of his RS project would be. The requirement was that he should research opinions on some religious issue, write up the results and offer his own reflections. Because it was fresh in his mind, he talked about the previous night's discussion, stressing

What To Do?

how intriguing it had been, and how difficult. Indeed, the members of the Youth Fellowship had found themselves offering contrary advice to the office worker, with one girl saying, 'The important thing is what Jesus would have done,' and another commenting, 'Don't be daft! How can you know? He was a man, anyway, and never had to answer the telephone.' Matthew acknowledged that he had been irritated when someone had said, 'Pray about it, and you will be shown what's right,' and even more annoyed when a younger boy still in the fifth form had commented, 'Oh, go and get another job.'

'So', said his teacher, 'What did you say?'

'I said,' replied Matthew, 'that sometimes one has to cover up the truth a bit, like the doctor who, for fear of a regression, doesn't tell someone plainly that they are dying. But one can't go on like that for long. If one does, one's own ideas of truth get blurred and one becomes an habitual deceiver. So, if she feels that that is happening to her or the situation is unbearable, she should look for another job.'

'And supposing she does, and in another office the same thing happens?'

'I really don't know,' replied Matthew, after a long pause.

'And how does being a Christian make any difference?'

'I'm not sure. It must make a difference somehow or other, mustn't it? Perhaps it gives her more strength in refusing to do what is wrong?'

And so the project was born. It was agreed that Matthew would try to find out how Christians sort out what to do, especially when facing tricky moral dilemmas, and what their values are. He would enquire among his contemporaries, in the church which he and his family attended, and from others who were willing to be known as Christians and churchgoers. And he wasted no time in getting started.

When the evening meal had been cleared away, he cornered his mother in the kitchen with an apparently innocent question:

The Project Conceived

'Mum, you don't mind if people refer to you as a Christian, do you?' His mother looked wary. 'No, of course not. But why ask? Do you want me to be the guinea pig for another of your schemes?'

'It's my RS project. It's school-work and I need to take it seriously,' Matthew replied. 'I'm enquiring how Christians decide moral matters. So how about you? Do you ask yourself what Jesus would do or use Jesus' teaching in any special way? Or do you follow the Ten Commandments and the Old Testament laws? What do you do about all that teaching? Do you compromise with any of it?'

His mother sat down and thought. 'Let's start,' she said, 'with Jesus' teaching. I don't manage to do exactly as he teaches in the Sermon on the Mount. I'm simply not sure about forgiving people who go on and on wronging me. I don't think I have anyone I could call an enemy but, if I had, I would find it hard to love them. And, perhaps because I value my security too much, I need a steady job and a stable home life. If pressed, I admit that some of Jesus' teaching is impossible for me, but I can't say that I've worried much about that before now.'

'Well, Jesus wasn't married, was he? And he didn't have to run a home and rear a family like you. And, after all, nobody threatens to put you on a cross, do they?'

'No, but that sounds too easy a get-out. I can't say that, because Jesus wasn't a ward manager in the NHS like me, what he said is irrelevant, or that, because I have a husband and three children to look after, I can forget him. I can't, and I never want to. He was the Ideal Man, I suppose, or the Ideal Person, the one who was totally open to God. I don't want to explain him away. He's far too important for that. And his parables and sayings intrigue me and challenge me, so that I can't get away from them, and I find inspiration in them. But don't ask me precisely what difference that makes to me, or whether for that reason I'm better than anyone else.'

What To Do?

'What about the church and its teaching?'

'I don't know. I'm not sure precisely what our church teaches about lots of things. I think it allows some abortions and re-marriage in church after a divorce, and that, unlike the Roman Catholics, it doesn't ban contraception. But, so far as I can see, it leaves us to make up our own minds on most things, and doesn't have a party line. It used to be strongly opposed to drink and gambling, but seems to have made fewer pronouncements on those issues recently. I'm glad there's no indoctrination. That would go against the grain with me.'

And so the discussion went on, untidily, with his mother looking uncertain about 'conscience' and some of the other terms Matthew threw into the ring. 'I'm happier to talk about my duty', his mother said, 'because that's fairly well defined when you work in the NHS, and we hang the Patients Charter up prominently in the Ward.' She was keen on the Ten Commandments, but cagey about some of the other injunctions in the Bible. 'Paul said that women should keep quiet in church,' said Matthew, 'but your sister is a Local Preacher, and you have never objected to that.' 'I think he was a bit old-fashioned there,' she remarked. 'Then what about all the other things he said? Can you pick and choose which to listen to?' 'Well, you have to. Some of his ideas were ridiculous. He said, for example, that women should cover their heads in church – and I can't stand hats! Moreover, I don't 'Honour the Emperor', as the Bible commands, because I haven't got one to honour – and, in any case, lots of emperors seem to me to have been thoroughly dishonourable people.'

At this point, father came in wanting a coffee, it being ten o'clock, and the discussion broke up, but not before Matthew had announced, 'Mum says that she picks and chooses which bits of the Bible to listen to.' 'Of course she does,' his father replied. 'We all do – but not randomly. We choose according to certain principles.' 'Like what?' 'Well, like, "Does this ring true to the way Jesus lived and taught?", "Is this sensible?", "Is

The Project Conceived

it practicable?", "Is it fair on everyone involved?", "What if everyone did it?" and "Is it the way of love?"' Then everyone went to bed, and Matthew was left wondering if he had bitten off more than he could chew.

Questions for discussion

1. What advice would you give to a young Christian who was ordered at work to tell lies on the telephone?

2. Do you pick and choose which bits of the Bible's moral teaching to listen to? If so, by what principles?

2

Youth Fellowship

On the whole Matthew didn't feel that the Youth Fellowship meeting went well. He came away with an impressive sheaf of notes but a sense of disappointment. The group seemed more interested in whether moral decisions were 'great' than in how they were made. Try as he might, he couldn't keep their attention on the underlying assumptions or the methods of the arguments that people were using. If he asked, 'Why do we approve of such-and-such but disapprove of other stances?' the replies tended to be a shrug of the shoulders and a comment like, 'It's obvious. Everyone knows that.'

Yet in the midst of this muddle there had been useful moments. One of the quieter, more thoughtful girls had told him that he should accept that his conscience was the 'voice of God inside'. If he relied on conscience, as she did, he wouldn't be so anxious. In support of this claim, she cited an incident from last week. A new and rather brash boy had joined their class and at once invited her out for a date. Something told her to be careful, and she declined. At once he turned nasty, insulted her and stalked off, saying he could get 'whoever he wanted'. A friend then told her that she had had a lucky escape, since he had a terrible temper but could turn on the charm to get what he wanted. 'See?' she said to Matthew, 'You always listen to the voice inside, and then God guides you.'

Another illuminating moment came over coffee afterwards. One of the leaders, a young man in his early twenties who was known to be 'rather serious, but OK really', drew him aside and talked earnestly about the Bible. 'We can never know what to do unless we study the scriptures first,' he said, 'for they are the blueprint from God, the Maker's instructions for us. If I'm ever stumped, I say a prayer for guidance, then open the scriptures carefully and read the passage I'm led to. I don't have to do this often – about once every six months, I suppose.

Youth Fellowship

But it has never failed me. I have always been given the right word from God.'

Matthew asked for an example of how the method worked. 'When I first came to live in this area two years ago,' he was told, 'I had to decide which church to join. I couldn't be a Catholic, and when I saw on the Parish Church's notice board that the Vicar was called 'Father so-and-so', I knew that wasn't the place for me either. So it had to be the Baptists, the Methodists or the Community Church. I didn't want to go round them all like a wine-taster, so I prayed about it and said, "Lord, lead me where you want me to be." Then I opened the scriptures and the Lord showed me the text, "and write them on the doorposts of your house and on your gates," referring to his Word. So then I knew.' 'Knew what?' asked Matthew. 'I knew the Lord's test. I was to go and see which church had his Word displayed outside. And when I looked one Saturday evening, only this church had a text on its notice board. That's why I'm here – where God wants me to be.'

When Matthew got home he felt increasingly uneasy. What was it that made the group have such forceful opinions? Some things were scorned with fury – racism, hypocrisy, injustice, homelessness, bigotry. Other things, by contrast, were reckoned to be morally trivial – demands for high wages, fast driving, 'playing around a bit' sexually, drug-taking, fiddling the income tax. Why should some things be patently wrong, and not others? There seemed little rhyme or reason to it.

And yet – there had been exceptions. One person trusted conscience absolutely. But surely, he thought, one's conscience, not being perfect, could sometimes be wrong. And granted that two people were equally sincere, one person's conscience could say one thing and the other's the opposite. That was clear in the case of abortion. Some denounced it utterly, others supported it, while still others said it was all right in rather special cases. But all parties appealed to 'conscience'. So where did that get us? And

What To Do?

couldn't one trace in a person's so-called 'inner voice' something of their upbringing? A middle-class Englishman seemed to have a different inner voice from that of a working-class Irishman.

Then there was the question of the Bible as a supernatural guide. The more Matthew thought about it, the more doubtful about the notion he became. Jesus, he reckoned, never told us to look into the Bible like that. And about very modern dilemmas – like those related to genetic engineering and the cloning of animals – where, he asked himself, does the Bible say anything pertinent? Then his pondering took another turn. Don't people tend to have a group morality, in solidarity with the people they most associate with? The Youth Fellowship seemed to have one, as did the Sixth Form at school. And maybe professional people who read *The Times* and sometimes attend the Parish Church are as predictable in their moral attitudes as readers of *The Sun* who frequent pubs and enjoy football matches?

Then another query sprang to mind. Some members of the Youth Fellowship had said, 'It's up to you, isn't it? You must do your own thing.' At school and elsewhere, he had often heard similar things. An uncle, a journalist by trade and very sceptical about the church, was often saying, 'You must choose your own values for yourself. Don't let you parents do it for you. Be a real person in your own right. You won't expect them to tell you which party you should vote for at the next general election, so why let them influence you about your other moral values?' At the time, he had failed to think of a reply to this kind of advice, but now he wondered whether it was a way of avoiding the kind of hard thinking which he ought to be doing. After all, what good reason did he have not to listen carefully to his parents? He was full of respect for them and their faith and all that they both stood for, and he often hoped that he could be like them. In any case, was it really credible that moral values are purely relative? Did one choose them idly, like selecting different brands of soup from the supermarket shelf? That seemed to trivialize morality.

Questions for discussion

1. Is one's conscience an adequate guide in the moral life? If not, what should we do about it?

2. How can we be sure that our moral judgments are Christian when so many are clearly moulded by the social group to which we belong?

3

The Businessman

Matthew had early decided that he ought to discuss his project with a Christian who was a businessman. He was unsure why. Maybe because his introduction to Marxism had told him that capitalists are the source of all evil! In addition, to Matthew's intense irritation, the young man next-door, who had assured him three years ago that going into business meant making a lot of money, was now, aged 24, driving a flashy sports car and being more swell-headed than ever. Matthew, then, had deep suspicions of businessmen, but his father had chatted with a steward at their church who ran a computer sales business, and a visit had been arranged.

Nothing at the meeting went according to expectations. To begin with, this businessman didn't look at all like a wicked capitalist. He was small, lively, and dressed in casual clothes and shirt sleeves. He sat in an airy office with six others, all looking very relaxed; and everyone used Christian names, as if in a country club. The 'boss' went and got a cup of tea and a biscuit, showed him quickly round the workplace, introducing him to everyone there, and then said 'OK. Now for your project. What do you want to know?'

Matthew managed to say, 'What are the moral obligations of a Christian like you in business?'

'My first obligation is to Jesus Christ. In everything I do, in every part of my life – home, leisure, family – my first loyalty is always to him. But I reckon that he then says to me, "Show your loyalty to me: in your home, by the way you love your wife and children; in the community, by honouring your neighbours and trying to improve both your local society and your nation; in your business, by dealing honourably with three groups of people – your workers, your shareholders and the people you trade with."'

'I thought,' said Matthew, 'that your first duty was to make as much money as possible, provided that you do it fairly.'

'Some businessmen will say that. But I have never believed it. In fact, when I did a university Business Studies course a few years ago, we were told to be suspicious of that approach. It makes the shareholders into little gods, and therefore too important. My own view is that the three main obligations are more or less equal. They balance each other nicely and prevent regarding profit as the only aim that matters. In this way, indeed, they also square with the New Testament's warnings about making money into the sort of God that Jesus calls "mammon". And, as always, Jesus is right – spot on, in fact!'

'But if you don't make a profit, the business fails, the workers are out of a job, the shareholders have lost their money, and you have then let everyone down, including God.'

'True. The business must work, and it's part of my job to see that it does. If we become inefficient or careless or out-of-date, then slowly but surely we will go under. We have to be alive and alert, looking forward all the time. That's only sensible management. What I'm saying is that, once you have got the management style right, you don't then say, "Now let's see how we can make the greatest possible profit," but "How can we improve the profits and the work you all do, perhaps by employing more people, and the service we give to our customers and through them to the world at large?" It's never just a matter of bigger profit, or bigger wages, for that matter.'

'Is there a difference between the ways in which you, as a Christian, treat your workers and the ways anyone else would?'

'Any enlightened manager wants to treat staff well, to respect their particular gifts and abilities, and to encourage them. Anyone who is on top of this sort of job, whether a Christian or not, will want to pay good wages, to see that there is good consultation, and so on. But for me, as a Christian, there is an extra bit of motivation. One doesn't just do these things to be

What To Do?

liked more or for the firm to be well thought of, but because one is answerable somehow to Christ.'

'So there is no noticeable difference?'

'Not at first, perhaps. But there is a different atmosphere in a place running on Christian principles. People are more at ease, tend to get on better together, are less competitive against each other. And there are other features of life here, deriving from my general philosophy, which are ultimately outworkings of my faith.'

'Such as?'

'We believe in openness. Everyone is entitled to know what decisions have been made, and as many people as possible share in making them. A few things have to be kept confidential – financial negotiations, information about our workers' previous employment, that sort of thing – but these are few. Every six months we share with the work-force the general state of the business, what the cash flow is like and any new development that is planned. Then there is the buying of our shares. Workers who have been with us for three years can start buying our shares at special rates. Without exception, they do. Those who have been here a longer time are now quite big shareholders.'

'A girl I know at church works in the offices of a supply company, but not in computers, like you. She answers the phone and often deals with complaints from customers. She is given strict orders to tell them things which she knows are plain lies. Could that happen here?'

'Never. Our people must always tell the truth. If we are to blame for letting someone down, we apologize on the phone and promise to get it put right at once.'

'Presumably you allow people to join a union?'

'That is a basic human right, and it's also the law of the land. You won't need much help from the union to negotiate any matters here, but I still encourage people to join. A strong union often helps other workers who may be struggling with

The Businessman

hard-nosed companies who don't care a jot about workers' rights. We all have a duty towards those workers too.'

'What about the sins Christians used to go on about? Drinking, smoking, gambling and so on.'

'Alcohol is not allowed here. Smoking isn't either, but the law says that we have to provide a place for smokers to use. We have a designated spot behind the warehouse, but nobody has ever used it yet. Gambling could only happen in the lunch break, and some of our office staff do the National Lottery together. We get a little mild swearing at times. All those things are trivial. The worst sins here would be dishonesty or disruptiveness. We get some jealousy sometimes. Not much. But that is human nature.'

Matthew went away disarmed. The place seemed so happy and purposeful. 'Surely,' he said to himself, 'not all businesses are like this?'

Questions for discussion

1. In your experience how common is a business like this one? How 'Christian' is it?

2. How enthusiastic should Christians be about trade unions?

4

The Scientists

Matthew wanted to interview a scientist, and his teacher arranged for him to visit a friend of his. Eric was a research worker in a fairly sophisticated food research institute, a young man in his early thirties, recently married. When Matthew arrived, Eric said, 'I know what it's all about. Can my wife join in? Julie's a chemist, working in a team developing special drugs. I'm a biologist mainly, investigating factory-produced foodstuffs.'

'What are they?' asked Matthew.

'Well, foods that you get in the shops nowadays have been processed before they reach you. Chocolate, for example, starts out as cocoa and goes through several production stages before it comes out as a Mars bar. We may be able to take easily-grown foods like wheat or turnips or potatoes or special grass, add some needed nutrition (through some fruits, for example), then dry the whole thing out and send it in compact form to the Third World. That could be quite cheap, and when they add water, hey presto: they have a meal which offers a first-rate diet, and whether or not the local harvest succeeds, people can be fed.'

'You mean that you could solve the problem of world hunger?'

'Not for the foreseeable future. But we could make things very much easier for Africa, when there is bad drought, or for China, when floods devastate a region, or for big cities, when their slums breed starvation and disease. So far the stuff we have made is pretty tasteless, and much too expensive. But the possibility of a breakthrough sooner or later makes the research worthwhile.'

'And what do you do, Julie?' Matthew asked.

'I'm a member of a research team working on drugs to help relieve asthma,' she replied. 'That probably sounds marvellous but for most of the time it's actually very dull. For example, we all spend hours doing routine work like reading research papers from all over the world. In addition, some of us concentrate on alleviating the side effects of drugs we already manufacture, while others work with our users, setting up tests with them and with their doctors. We have to get used to reams and reams of statistics.'

'But that means that both of you are doing research which will directly benefit lots of people. As Christians, you must find that very satisfying.'

'Neither of us would work at something that wasn't going to bring clear human benefit,' said Eric. 'And, yes, we are lucky with our jobs.'

'But we still have difficult problems to live with,' said Julie. 'Our drugs have to have very thorough testing, especially on animals like rats and rabbits. I hate going down to the section where the animals live – rows upon rows of them in cages, barely able to do anything except eat and sleep. None of them ever gets a chance to run anywhere. Some die after the first injection, some of them are listless and ill, and lots of them shrink away when anyone comes near. It's horrible, but necessary. Only when we are sure that something helps an animal can we risk it on a human being. Sometimes, before I go to bed, I think about all those poor animals trying to sleep. And I ask God to forgive me for giving them asthma. I reckon that God does, but I hate myself for what I've done.'

'Why, if it's necessary? And can't your faith help you?'

'Yes. My faith says I must never hate myself, because God can't hate me. But it's still horrid, and I have to train myself not to get too thick-skinned about it.'

'My problems come more from the likelihood of the firm being taken over,' said Eric. 'It happened recently, in fact, and half our workforce lost their jobs. One just has to keep calm, stop worrying overmuch, and trust that one's life will not be wrecked by it. One also has to learn how to be sympathetic to everyone involved and how to handle the bitterness of some of those who lose their jobs.

'Recently, I heard a preacher say that, if you make a Christian witness at work, many people come and confide in you and you know you are where God wants you to be. It doesn't happen like that to me. I get a lot of stick from two colleagues who are very cynical about faith and about the church. They would never want to share anything personal. Many of the others are very private people too. We are all young, well educated, and the sort who have never had it so good. We rarely get into deep conversation. People are afraid of it. Their general line is that moral values are all relative. You choose them for yourself and don't impose them on anyone else. So I have to be patient and quiet.'

'How do you decide what to do when you have a moral crisis – when, for example, you have to evaluate the lesser of two evils?' asked Matthew.

There was a long pause. Finally, Julie said, 'The most difficult moral problems for me have not been at work. When I was at university I was really bothered about relationships. There was a lot of peer pressure to regard it as light-hearted fun if you went to bed with someone. I never felt that to be right, and I was forced to sort out my ideas, especially about what love should be like. It made me much more tolerant of others. I concluded that you couldn't say that some young student jumping into bed with another was a grievous sin. But you could say that exploitation was, or self-righteousness. So I read the Bible in a new light, realizing that most moral issues involve not black and white, but shades of grey.'

Eric followed. 'I agree. Work is not too complex for me, and I don't get unduly bothered about it. But I find it hard to learn how to allocate our money well, and how to get on at church. Julie and I tithe our joint income, but I find that difficult and sometimes resent it. It's a good job that we have a firm rule about it. And as for the church, we have many tensions there. I

The Scientists

disagree with our minister. He is too narrow and, in my view, misleads the young people by trying to lay down the law too much. And then we have huge arguments in our Church Council, usually about money. I reckon that Paul teaches clearly that we have to be over-generous, but some of our leaders are always wittering on about saving for a rainy day. And I must admit that I don't get on very well with my parents; I never have. That bothers me. It doesn't seem Christian at all.'

Questions for discussion

1. Is Julie right in saying that moral issues are rarely 'black and white'? What effect should that have on our moral judgments?

2. Eric found the most difficult problems were over money, the church, and the family. Where do you find most difficulties?

5

The Mother

The Youth Fellowship leader suggested that Matthew should go and see her sister-in-law, a keen Christian who thought deeply about the issues he was exploring. When he went, he was told to call her Elaine, and listened whilst she explained that at present she didn't go out to work whilst her three children were young. 'It's God's will,' she said, 'so it's all right by me.'

Matthew got out his notebook and some prepared questions. 'How do you decide about moral matters?' he began. 'Do you try to obey Jesus' teaching literally all the time or do you compromise when that's impossible?'

'He never orders us to do the impossible,' she replied, 'and when he says things like "Turn the other cheek," he is giving an illustration of what love is like, not an order to slaves. His main commands are only two – to love God totally, and one's neighbour as oneself – and everything finally hangs on those.'

'But one can't teach children to turn the other cheek in the playground,' said Matthew, 'or they get bullied by other children. When I was six my Dad told me to stand up for myself and not be a wimp. So if I got hit, I hit back harder, and got on much better after that.'

'But what Jesus taught was for adults. At first children have to learn to be sturdy, as you say, but later they grow up and learn the adult ways of love. One has to prepare them for that, just as one doesn't start them off at school with astrophysics.'

'But what about giving to everyone who asks of you? Do you tell them to share their pocket-money now, and later, when they grow up, to share all their wages?'

'I teach them to be sensible, and always willing to share things. After all, Jesus doesn't require me to supply all the children in Abbey First School with pens and chocolate biscuits. All our obligations have boundaries.'

The Mother

'Supposing one of your children is naughty. Do you smack them?'

'Never. We will tell them off, or punish in some simple way like sending them to their bedroom for a few minutes. But we never use violence, even in a small way. It is against Jesus' whole style of living.'

'Suppose some child molester tried to grab one of your children?'

There was a long pause. 'I had hoped that you wouldn't ask that sort of question. It's every mother's nightmare. I would probably go mad and attack him like a tiger. I shudder to think about it. Fortunately we rarely have to face traumas like that in normal life.'

'What, then, are the really difficult issues which we do have?'

'In our experience the worst dilemma was when we had to sort out what to do for Greg's mother. She is nearly seventy-five, riddled with arthritis, and all on her own. Greg has one brother, but he's in India, so it was up to us. She could no longer live on her own, but we couldn't make room for her here, and I doubt whether I could nurse her adequately. We don't get on well; she's so interfering, and if she stays here, we can only stand a week at the most. I'm always asking God's forgiveness because I get so cross with her. She always refused to go into a home, but in the end the doctor was marvellous and persuaded her to go. She has settled in quite well and is now fairly happy. I think it was the most loving solution, and of course, if it is the most loving thing, then it is the right one, as the Bible teaches.'

'Do you think, then, that all Christian problems boil down in the end to sorting out the most loving thing?'

'Of course. That is the teaching of the Bible. Not at first in the Old Testament, when God's people were morally immature, living by "an eye for an eye and a tooth for a tooth". But God sent the prophets, and they were always pointing to something better – do justly, love mercy and walk humbly with your God. That's impressive. Then, when Jesus came, he took the best of all that remarkable tradition and perfected it. He both taught the way of love and lived it out perfectly.'

Matthew thought for a while and then said, 'I know that Jesus is often held up as an example to us. But surely he can only be one in a very limited way? We don't know anything about his time as a carpenter, so he can't be much of an example to workers. He didn't get married and have children, so he can't really be an example for parents. He didn't have to live in our developed society with its heavy drugs and porny videos and free condoms, so he can't be an example to young people today. Or can he?'

'Yes, he can, because he got the business of loving absolutely right, loving God and everyone else. That's the key thing, whether you are living on a Pacific Island in the eighteenth century or in Birmingham in the twenty-fifth. I see him as living the one really right and true life the world has ever known. That's why he is an example and an encouragement. We can't do without him, if we want to get a proper focus on the Christian life.'

'A focus?'

'Yes, we all need a marvellous example to copy. We don't need lots of laws or rules or good advice. We need great figures, saints, people about whom we find ourselves saying, "I wish I were like him or her." We call them "role models" nowadays. We can't possibly do without them. Parents should be good models for their children to copy; the older people at church should be good models for the younger ones to copy; and so on. But for everyone Jesus is the ideal model. And we should try to develop what Paul calls "the mind of Christ". I hope that my children feel that Greg and I try to do that, however often we fail.'

The Mother

Questions for discussion

1. Do we all need a marvellous example to copy? Can Jesus be the ideal role model for today?

2. Are Jesus' commands more like illustrations than laws to be carefully obeyed?

6

The Long Arm of the Law

'I was full of idealism at first,' he said. 'I'd been converted at a Billy Graham rally when I was seventeen, and when I joined the Force, I thought that my faith would make me a super copper and get me with ease through every possible problem. Then after three or four years I began to lose that first naïve enthusiasm and become cynical. And getting attacked and knocked about several times didn't help. You don't waste time, I can assure you, telling yourself to be kind and loving when some drunken villain is coming at you with a broken bottle. It's the law of the jungle then. So those years were bad. Sometimes I hated the job, and sometimes I found it unbearably frightening. But after about eight years someone suggested that I ought to put in for promotion. When I did, I was made up to Sergeant, and that was a turning point for me. I began to see everything differently.'

Matthew was relieved. A friend had arranged for him to visit this Police Sergeant who was an avowed Christian, and at first he had been apprehensive. But in beginning their conversation in this way, the policeman showed himself as kind and honest.

He went on, 'You see, the promotion showed that the Force had confidence in me, and as a result I began to think that my faith was making a difference and that other people noticed it. For instance, just before this I had been very troubled. One of my mates had broken the rules – I suppose we all do at times. He had lost his cool with a prisoner and had roughed him up. There was a formal complaint, and I was called in to testify about it. I found I couldn't do a cover-up by telling lies. After all, the ninth commandment forbids it. My mate got a reprimand and I thought that, since he could have been kicked out of the Force, he would be mad with me for not supporting him. But he came to me and said, "You did right. You told the truth, and I never ought to have expected anything different from you. I've learnt my lesson." After that, I felt much better about the whole episode. The respect of your mates is a great thing – in fact, you can't manage without it.'

'Are you saying that a policeman often breaks the rules?'

'No, but we are only human, and people often wind us up remorselessly. We can feel them trying it on, and going from one stage to another, hoping to make us snap. We have to get used to it, and learn how to cope.'

'So you see the worst in human nature.'

'Yes, we see a lot of rogues, a lot of people driven to crime by desperation, and a lot of evil people who have no compunction about what they're doing. But we also see the other side – people being generous, helpful, dedicated, trying hard to lift others up.'

'But what difference does it make if you are a Christian?'

'I think that it helps you to maintain the high standards expected in the Force. After all, good standards in any walk of life usually match up with what the Bible teaches, and policing is no different. One must show honesty, self-control, firmness, compassion – all those good qualities.'

'But what about the constant use of force? Jesus told us to turn the other cheek when attacked, to forgive those who wrong us, to give to everyone in need, to love our enemies, didn't he?'

'Those are the bits of the Bible which people sometimes throw at us. I can't get away from that teaching. It's always there as reminder of what the Lord practised himself. But that's not the whole of the Bible's teaching, is it? In Jesus' time the soldiers acted as a police force, and he never told a soldier to quit the army or throw away his shield. He even told his disciples to make sure that they had a sword, which every sensible man carried if he was going on a journey through some of the wild parts of the land. There is a place for defensive force. And later on Christians were taught, "For the Lord's sake accept the authority of every human institution, whether the emperor or governor, because they are sent to punish those who

What To Do?

do wrong." That's in I Peter, but people who don't know the Bible well usually ignore it.'

'So you think that a policeman's use of a truncheon or CS spray can be justified because in God's ordering of things they have a place?'

'Of course. Bible teaching doesn't require us to behave as if we are all in heaven already. It's designed for a world full of sinners. It isn't starry-eyed. If it were, it would be irrelevant.'

'Then are you saying that the use of force is quite OK?'

'No. It's an unfortunate necessity, always a last resort and something to be very careful about. A police officer is in a position of considerable power. He or she can, if necessary, summon all kinds of force, including sharpshooters. Power is always a source of temptation. It must not be abused, and Jesus' teaching is always there to remind us of that. In the same way, police officers can be tempted to notice some things and ignore others, or to go along with some characters and even get kick-backs from them. All those temptations are terribly strong, and the Lord is there to keep us determined not to succumb, and to keep the use of force within proper bounds.'

'Supposing you have a difficult moral dilemma. How does your faith help you to resolve it?

'Like what? I told you about my mate hoping for a cover-up. The plain teaching of the Bible was my strength in that case.'

'OK, supposing you catch a sixteen-year-old boy driving a car on a joyride. Then you discover that his father is someone important, like the Chief Constable, and your immediate boss suggests that you drop the whole thing and just give the lad a warning?'

'That wouldn't be fair or right. Driving like that is a serious matter. I would fall back on the plain biblical teaching that "God is no respecter of persons." God doesn't wink the eye because the offender is important, even if he be the king. Justice is what counts to God, and I would let that be my guide too. I would say that it wouldn't be just to treat that boy differently because of his father. In the end, it's wonderful how the Bible gives us the clues we need when facing a crisis or dilemma.'

Questions for discussion

1. In your experience do good standards, in any occupation or aspect of life, usually match up with what some parts of the Bible teach?

2. Since power and authority are always exposing their holders to temptation, what has been your experience of the appropriate ways of controlling power?

7

A Résumé

Matthew, having tried to put his thoughts into some sort of order, shared them with his teacher. He explained that his various interviews had tended to run along by-passing many of his prepared questions, but opening up new issues. At the same time, he acknowledged his good fortune in being able to talk to thoughtful, articulate people who, even when presented with searching questions, had been willing to be frank and open with him.

He reported, too, that for many people the setting of their work supplied its own code of behaviour. For example, nursing has its professional standards; police procedures are legally defined; businessmen refer to something called 'established business practice'; and scientific research is built on agreed methods. Unless, therefore, there were good reasons not to, the first task of the Christian or any other worker in these areas seemed to be to comply with the relevant code.

The teacher asked if this were a good or bad thing. Matthew thought long and finally said, 'I suppose it must be a good thing. Those codes, developed over years and years, must represent the experience of countless numbers of people.'

The teacher asked, 'Is the same true of all our moral ideas? Have all come down through centuries of experience and testing?'

'I suppose so. I've never thought of it like that before. But, even so, one can't agree with everything from the past or there would be no new ideas and we would still think it right to burn witches, wouldn't we?'

'True, but you sense, I think, that your young contemporaries don't see it like that. Your Youth Fellowship has a sort of code, but you find them, so far as I can tell, a bit superficial and not very aware of the past.'

A Résumé

'Yes, but I may be too hard on them. How often do they get the chance for serious moral discussion? In some lessons at school, like RS, if they are lucky. In the Youth Fellowship, if they go to church. And perhaps at home if, like me, they can discuss things with their parents. Otherwise it's merely a matter of talking in the same peer group, which is really very narrow.'

'What about the TV? Doesn't it influence people tremendously? The soaps and dramas, for example. They may not stage great moral debates but they often show people having to make vital decisions on matters of life and death.'

'Yes, but my Mum says they have to make things dramatic in order to keep viewing figures up. You rarely see a happy marriage because an unhappy one looks more interesting, and a bit of adultery is always exciting. But there's also a special sort of "political correctness" at work, an unwritten assumption that moral values are subjective and that each person is free to select their own. People who believe in objective moral values are usually presented as prejudiced or bigoted.'

'OK. But now tell me: in the people you have seen, what difference, if any, can you ascribe to their faith?'

'Well, the businessman's attitudes and the application of his principles seemed to produce an unusually relaxed atmosphere in his workplace. And some people, like the young mother, are much clearer about important issues because of their faith. The Sergeant knew his Bible jolly well and that seemed to make him much more certain and assured – rather like my parents, in fact! Then there's my friend who says that her conscience guides her. Though only 17, she strikes me as mature and balanced, and different. In general, perhaps faith gives you a firmer hold on the really important things in life and, consequently, you don't get rattled so easily by problems or carried along by the crowd.'

'You mentioned people who rely a lot on the Bible, and you were very critical of one of them for whom the posters outside and a text in the Old Testament were decisive when it came to

What To Do?

deciding which church he would join. Is the Bible a help, or does it, if used uncritically, make people naïve?'

'The occasional person is naïve,' said Matthew, 'but by no means everyone I talked to. What strikes me is that, if in making moral decisions we have to take the Bible with supreme seriousness, most Christians are ruled out. They can't spend all their time studying it, and they may not have the sort of memory that the Sergeant, who could quote texts about almost anything, relied on. The young mother had a point, though, when she spoke about "doing the most loving thing".'

'But is it a true guide for Christian moral judgment? Or is it deceptively over-simple?'

'I'll think more about it. I also want to ask more about Jesus. Some people didn't even mention him. My Mum did, but others seemed to be able to get along without quoting him at all or had found all sorts of ways round his teaching. Is that legitimate? I sensed that they all too easily resorted to compromise.'

'Well, is compromise such a bad thing? Or is it inevitable?'

'I thought it was meant to be a dirty word for Christians.'

'I've never said so.'

'Oh. You surprise me. I'll have to enquire more, I suppose. But can I mention something else? Hardly anyone quoted the teaching of their church. My Mum said she didn't know what her church had to say on many of the things we debate at home. Surely every church ought to have a considered view, and to pass it on to its members?'

'The Roman Catholic Church most definitely has, and so have most of the small churches. Mainstream Protestant denominations tend to be a bit more vague because their churches are more liberal and include people with a wide range of views. That means that most people only remember the negative things they have said, like, "Go easy on the drink and on this and that and don't enjoy yourself too much." You must widen your enquiries, especially by talking to a Catholic.'

A Résumé

'You wanted me to ask what people do when faced with moral dilemmas. That isn't very clear yet, but the answers I've so far gathered seem consistent with their general approaches. Perhaps that's inevitable, but I'll press on. What do I do next?'

'I want you to go now to people whose jobs, or whose interests, have made them think more and maybe read more about moral issues. As a result, they can perhaps be described as "moral experts". I've made all the arrangements for you. None of these people is a highbrow academic, and even the one who teaches philosophy is a down-to-earth character! You will enjoy this.'

Questions for discussion

1. Is compromise with Jesus' teaching inevitable in this fallen world? Have you had to make such a compromise recently?

2. Does the teaching of your church matter very much to you? Should it? Should it be communicated with more urgency?

8

The Doctor

'What matters most, if we are to behave properly as Christians, is that we have a well-formed conscience and a good will. That's what all the teaching and worship of the church should help us to develop.' He looked quizzically at Matthew, who simply wanted him to go on. 'I'm a doctor, and I try to be as effective as I can. But ninety per cent of my time I'm no different from any other GP wanting to do a good job. One of our first needs is to keep up-to-date with modern medicine and treatments. Another is to keep fit. I see too many of my colleagues working or worrying themselves to bits, and it makes me shudder. Then one has to maintain a genuine interest in people, never getting bored by them or thinking, "Oh, how dull. Here's another arthritis." I suppose my faith helps with all those needs, though not very directly. But it certainly does help when one looks at the deepest things, like a good conscience.'

'What do you mean by that?' asked Matthew. 'I thought that conscience was the voice inside that makes one feel a bit rotten after one has been bad, a sort of moral hangover.'

'No, no, no,' replied the Doctor. 'One's conscience is the sort of moral compass that we all have deep down, pointing to what is truly good, to the moral law God has built into all human life. It's not simply the pain one feels when one has sinned, and not something that only Christians have. The difference in being a Christian is in the sort of training one tries to give it, so that it is tuned to the very best things in life.'

'You seem to be speaking about a moral law. Do you mean the ten commandments, or something like them?'

'I mean something bigger, although the commandments are a part of it. I mean God's will for every individual, for our society, for the world as a whole. It's not the same as all the teaching in the Bible put together, for that was given over hundreds of years and isn't always consistent. One needs help, therefore, from the contemporary church in order to see how God wants us to live today.'

'Are you saying, then, that the teaching of the church is more important than that in the Bible?'

'Yes and no. The church's teaching is based on the Bible, but when we read scripture we choose the bits that fascinate us most. We hardly ever read the whole lot. And then we argue like mad about what we derive from it. You must have noticed that. One Christian says one thing after reading some texts, another says something different after reading others. Who can say who is right? We need the church to help us sort it out, And another thing. When one has read the whole Bible, one has only just reached the third century. The Bible stops, about 1700 years ago. It can't offer guidance on the scores of questions that have arisen since then. So the church and the way the Spirit keeps inspiring her are vitally important.'

'Are you thinking of modern problems like organ transplants and genetic engineering and sophisticated drugs and treatments?'

'Yes, amongst other things. To get my conscience right on all sorts of new issues the Bible is of little help, and I need the massive wisdom of the church, and all the brains and expertise it can summon. That all gets passed down through prayer and through the teachings of the Holy Father, the Pope.'

'So his words are more important than those in the Bible?'

'No. It doesn't work like that. We never set one against the other. They support each other, like our two legs when we walk. The Pope would never teach something contrary to the Bible. On the other hand, we recognize that originally the church had to decide what the Bible was, which books were to be included in the canon and which excluded. Without the church we couldn't have a Bible which we could regard as the Word of God for us. And without the Holy Father that Word couldn't be kept fresh for us now.'

What To Do?

'In what ways have the Pope's recent pronouncements been helpful to you?'

'He has assessed very clearly the issues of divorce, abortion, homosexuality, contraception, euthanasia, and sterilization. All Catholics have been alerted to what is wrong in them. Such teaching guides me in my work almost every day, whether helping Catholics or others.'

'Right at the beginning you said something about both a good conscience and a good will. What did you mean by that second phrase?'

'One should always be seeking with all one's energy and desire what is good – not what will be easiest, most popular or most pleasurable, but "the good". That is what we want more than anything else. When other Christians say they want to do "God's will" they're saying the same thing but using different words. But one must have a pure intention so that God can work with us to produce what is truly good.'

'And if you are facing a serious moral conflict? How do you then know what to do? Faced by several good things, one cannot aim for them all and a choice has to be made.'

'Medical practice is full of such issues, and that's why the church's teaching is so necessary. If the worst comes to the worst, I talk over the dilemma with other Catholics, especially a priest.'

'All right, take something not primarily a medical problem. Suppose your mother-in-law is a widow, getting frail and needing a lot of help. She hates the idea of living in an old people's home and wants, if all else fails, to live with your family. Yet that too is impracticable. How do you know what then to do?'

'I wouldn't rush into a decision. I would talk over the situation with all parties, with good friends and a priest. If one prayed honestly and genuinely opened oneself to God and his grace, slowly but surely the answer would come.'

The Doctor

Matthew finally left, rather taken aback by the different sort of talk he had experienced. For he realized, when he got home, that they had never once talked about Jesus, never even mentioned his name. How odd!

Questions for discussion

1. Can we conceive ourselves needing 'the massive wisdom of the church?' If so, how would we expect to get it?

2. Is it your experience that, given time, every moral dilemma is clearly resolved?

9

The Lecturer

'You must realize that the average English person is simply a utilitarian,' he said, 'unless, that is, they think that everyone should choose whatever morals they prefer, that no moral ideas ought to be especially encouraged, and that therefore all moral talk is a waste of time: a view that goes down well in a society which isn't training itself to think seriously about these things any more.'

'What is a "utilitarian"?' asked Matthew.

The lecturer groaned. 'I thought that you would have at least a bit of moral knowledge in your head! What do they teach at your school? Ever heard of Plato or Aristotle? Hume or Kant? No, I thought not. You are taught the facts about this and that and how to operate gadgets, but never how to think. We will end up a nation of technicians and finance clerks, with nobody having a clue how to reflect about life.'

'I wouldn't mind studying philosophy,' said Matthew, 'but it isn't an option at our school. I've heard of the names of the people you mentioned, but I've never studied their writings. And I'm sorry but I don't know what it means to be a "utilitarian".'

The lecturer sighed again. 'In Western Europe and America "utilitarianism" is probably the most common ethical theory, propounded first by Locke, then by John Stuart Mill, then by Bentham. It's attractive, if you don't probe too much. It holds that what is morally right is what yields the most happiness for the greatest number. Look at the average TV play and you soon come across the sentiment, plus the fad word of today, "fulfilment". "I must fulfil myself," says the hero, and it is assumed that whatever produces fulfilment is justified and will make him happy.'

'I suppose,' said Matthew, 'that it depends on what happiness is meant to be. It's different for different people. One of my sisters simply loves dancing, but it bores me stiff.'

The Lecturer

'Quite. The theory assumes – quite wrongly, in my view, not least for the reason that you mention – that somehow or other one can calculate degrees of happiness. It also tends – and this appeals to our individualistic age – to leave out wider considerations and to neglect what you might call the "general good of society". According to this theory, for example, you could argue that most drugs should be legalized, since in this way more people would be made happier. But you wouldn't be bound to consider what sort of society such action would promote or the dangers that would face the weak and vulnerable. The theory, in short, is too limited to the individuals immediately involved and, like today's politics, tends to be short-termist.'

'But suppose someone is only happy when making others suffer? What about child molesters? One can't argue, surely, that their happiness should be encouraged?'

'No, of course not. If you take the theory too rigidly, you end up justifying perverse and wicked behaviour. But, more importantly, it's grounded in an over-optimistic assessment of human nature. Wickedness is unusual, it holds, and for the most part can be cured by proper enlightenment.'

'But there must be other theories around as well?'

'Yes. Some people argue that moral talk is only about your feelings. And some say that agonizing about moral decisions is pointless because all our actions are determined by our physical make-up. And then there is, or was, Marxism. Whatever in the long run will hasten the Great Revolution and get the wicked capitalists off the backs of the heroic workers is right – and anything goes, violence, trickery, murder, slave camps. The end is what matters, and human lives can be sacrificed for it without compunction. Horrible!'

'The end justifies the means?'

'Precisely. The Marxist lives – or dies – by that conviction. Nowadays most thinkers would say that of course the end is one of the factors that justifies an action, but that some means and some ends are always unworthy and therefore immoral. They would add that the means used tend to determine the end achieved.'

'None of the people I have interviewed have talked much about any of those issues. Maybe that's because they were all Christians? They have been more concerned with a good will, or a good intention, or doing God's will, and some of them have been strong on the Bible.'

'Fair enough. Christians have made a very important contribution by stressing right motives and a good will. Perhaps because of his Christian upbringing, Kant, one of the greatest philosophers of recent times, stressed the good will and wanted individuals so to act that, if everyone else did the same thing in similar circumstances, the general good would be served. And Roman Catholics have always stressed the good will and our duty to cultivate certain virtues through which it can be realized. It's not a bad starting-point, and the Bible soon becomes relevant and teaches what the best virtues are.'

'I haven't heard much mention of what you call "the virtues".'

'You will. The Greeks paid particular attention to certain key virtues which, in their view, it was important for individuals to acquire. Recently some important moral philosophers have become exasperated with certain types of moral discussion which, they say, have left the Western world in a mess. They are referring to debates which have encouraged everyone to regard morals as a big supermarket in which you choose what turns you on. In such a situation, they argue, we need to recover the idea that certain virtues matter profoundly and can lead to the good life. Christians have been fairly happy with this development. They may not go along with exactly the virtues that Aristotle commended, but they approve of the general idea. And they notice that Bible writers like Paul often string together a great list of virtues and tell Christians to "put them on". It's almost as if adopting them is like putting on a new set of clothes.'

'Are you saying that major moral philosophers today are arguing in a similar way to the Bible?'

'Yes, some are. Many are still discussing linguistic questions like what you mean when you call an action "good", and all that sort of thing. But some of shrewdest have said, "Let's get back to substantial moral thinking and talk about the virtues". One reason may be that today the best moral thinkers are not starry-eyed about human nature. We know how utterly evil individuals and nations can become. Films about the Holocaust are still being produced, and we hear about ethnic cleansing even in Europe itself, the cradle of modern liberal ideas. So the need is to be soberly realistic about human nature.'

Questions for discussion

1. Is the average English person a 'utilitarian'? In what ways is this likely to be good or bad for society?

2. What virtues do you think Christians should encourage?

10

The Minister

'I don't think I was ordained to teach morality,' said the minister, 'but to help the church to do its constant job, pointing people to God, offering the best worship it can, serving the local community, and spreading the Christian truth around.'

'But the church has a special view on most moral issues, surely?'

'Probably, but it isn't my first job to go round telling everyone what they should do or believe and what the church says about everything under the sun. I'm not a judge or a lecturer or even a teacher, but an encourager and witness.'

'All right,' said Matthew. 'Perhaps then I should be asking you what sort of morality you encourage?'

The minister shook his head. 'I'm still not happy with the idea that being a minister makes me some sort of expert on morality. Moral encouragement is only part of my job because Christian behaviour is a by-product of giving priority to Jesus Christ and trying to live the Christian life.'

He paused. Matthew thought that he was being unduly defensive. He had distinctly heard him say from the pulpit last Sunday, 'Racism is a sin. Stamp it out.' That seemed to Matthew to be plain moral direction and, because most preachers, in his view, were far too vague about these issues, he had been delighted to hear it. So he protested, 'But you said clearly last Sunday that we should have nothing to do with racism because it is a sin.'

'Yes, I did. But if you remember, the theme of the sermon was the good news that God makes us all special but different, and has no truck with the barriers we bring into the human family. So snobbery is a sin, and racism, and blind national pride. The moral bits were the outworking of the good news, which was what I most stressed.'

The Minister

'OK, but I thought that the "moral bits" were great. Most preachers are never as clear, and I often wonder why they tend to be so negative. Don't do this, don't do that, especially if it's something that everyone enjoys. They seem to be saying, "Don't listen to the modern world, but remember what was taught when the chapel was built a hundred years ago."'

'You're being a bit hard on us preachers. When we do our job properly, we will be saying: "Look to God. Look to Jesus. Listen to God's Word. Get your bearings for life like that. Then let's strive for all sorts of good, turn our backs on all sorts of evil, and have the ability to spot the difference." If you approved of my denouncing racism, you must surely agree that the best way to get to that point is to begin with God's truth, as I tried to do.'

'Let's start again. What sort of morality do you want the church to encourage? Should we stick firmly by the Ten Commandments?'

'They are only a beginners' guide, and by no means the last word in the Christian's equipment. They were first formulated in a far-off time and culture and are mainly negative. I gather that you don't like too many "Don'ts". On the whole Jesus was far more positive. He kept enthusing about what the Kingdom of God is like and urging us to try living like that. We should do the same today.'

'I interviewed a Roman Catholic doctor recently, a very dedicated man. He never mentioned Jesus once, but talked a lot about the Pope. You say, though, that it is Jesus we should talk most about.'

'Christians differ. My views may be different from those of the minister in the church down the road. Most Protestants, while sharing a general way of tackling moral issues, don't lay down firm positions but permit considerable freedom. The Catholics don't. They believe that the Pope is truly guided to teach the right views on matters of faith and morals. There are advantages with that. Wherever you go in the world you know that the Catholics will be opposing abortion or birth control, whereas some Protestants do and some don't.'

'But what about the omission of any reference to Jesus?'

'I was coming to that. Roman Catholics have a slightly different way of approaching morality from us. They first ask the question: "What is it like to be a person and to have moral obligations?" Then they ask: "How can the great gifts of faith, hope and love be ours too, so that our morality is fully Christian and draws strength from God?" Protestants usually don't begin like that. We tend to ask: "What does the Bible teach us about the morally good life?" And then we follow that up with: "How does Jesus help us live it?" The first approach, therefore, may barely mention Jesus, whereas the second is bound to do so.'

'I find that confusing. Why don't all Christians agree about the way to consider morality? Surely they should?'

'Yes, it would seem better if we did, but the plain fact is that we don't, any more than Protestants agree when they turn to the Bible. Indeed, the plain fact is that various approaches are offered to us within the Bible itself. It is as if God isn't wanting us to be too rigid in our moral thinking and is saying to us "Come at these issues in various ways."'

'Does this result in a situation where our own church leaves all moral judgment to the individual? My Mum thinks so, and that pleases her, since she wouldn't take kindly to being told what to do!'

'Our church helps us to form our convictions in lots of ways, but mainly by its whole life of worship and prayer and devotion. It also generates talk and reports and teaching notes and discussion papers on many things, and has occasional campaigns on specific issues.

Moreover, it issues formal statements on matters like euthanasia or gambling, but we aren't sworn to agree with them. The statements offer guidance rather than claim total adherence. As a result of all this, it is difficult for any church member not to be aware of our obligations to the poor, for example, both at home and overseas. Such matters are almost part of the air we breathe.'

'Supposing you have to resolve an acute moral dilemma. How do you do it?'

'In all these matters there are four sources of help I go to: the Bible, the teaching of the church, the general experience of most other Christians, and my reason. In addition, I have to think and pray hard, keep a sense of proportion, and not get flustered or take the easiest way out. Then, as I hold the claims of Jesus before me, somehow or other the Spirit edges me a certain way.'

'And has that often happened to you?'

After a long silence, the minister answered: 'Once I had an awful decision to make. I was due to be married in six weeks' time, and bit by bit every nerve in my body told me it was wrong. Somehow the Bible gave me the courage to face up to it, although I had been hiding from that truth for weeks. So I did something which may appear very cruel: I broke off the engagement. Much, much later I began to see what a mercy that was for both of us. I'm not sure how I decided it, but it was right.'

Questions for discussion

1. What part should the church and its ministers play in moral education?

2. Is it a weakness or a strength that Christians differ about morality?

11

Ethics in the Old Testament

Matthew told his teacher about these latest interviews, and said 'I feel more ignorant every time I talk to someone about all this, and especially if they mention the Bible.'

'Right,' was the reply. 'Let's start with the Old Testament. What ideas does it have about ethics?'

'We learned the Ten Commandments in Sunday School. And of course I know some of the stories, like David and Goliath, but I can't see what help that is to us today.'

'The basic idea running throughout the Old Testament books is that God has a good purpose for our lives and is always trying to make it clear to us. God, and God alone, is the source of our moral obligations, and he isn't remote or silent. He speaks through teachings and through all his helping, saving activities. But – two warnings to us. First, at that time all sorts of moral obligation were bundled together, with little distinction between right behaviour in worship, in farming, in family life, in business. Secondly, some of the bundle is frankly abhorrent now, since it was even believed that God commanded genocide and sheer brutality. Every right-thinking person should recoil from it. Consider Deuteronomy 6.1–6, for example, or the law of revenge in Deuteronomy 19.21. It's revolting!'

'So we have to pick and choose what to honour and what to ignore?'

'Yes, but not in an arbitrary way. We will discuss that later. You need to grasp that there are three main forms in which God's will is set out in the Old Testament. They are not in conflict but lie alongside each other, roughly corresponding to the three sections of law, prophets and writings into which the Jews divided their scriptures. In the first – chiefly the first six books and then some historical ones – God teaches mainly through law or commandment. Some of this material is very detailed, and the Jews reckoned that there were 248 positive laws and 365 negative ones. The good person, they held, tries to know them all and obey them gladly. The Ten Commandments come into this collection.'

'And we select them as the most helpful of the lot?' asked Matthew.

'Yes, often. But it is well to note that they are hardly ever mentioned in the rest of the Old Testament, and not much in the New. The second form is the prophetic writings, roughly the last third of the whole Old Testament, from Isaiah to Malachi. They concentrate on God's character. He has made a covenant with his people and they are under obligation to keep their side of it. This means being in some ways like God, so that we too should be holy and righteous, as God is, and we too should practise mercy and justice, because God does. This radically different and much more demanding idea is summed up in Micah 6.8: "What does the Lord require of you but to do justice and to love kindness and to walk humbly with your God?" If you asked "Why?", they would say that's the only fitting way to respond to the marvellous God who deals with us and wants us to learn from him.'

'I thought,' said Matthew, 'that the prophets were preachers who were always condemning what was going on and predicting the gloomiest possible future.'

'What a half-baked idea!' replied his teacher. 'The prophets had this keen awareness of God's involvement in everything that was happening all over the world. They knew all too well that, if one turns one's back on God, everything can go appallingly wrong. But they weren't astrologers or pessimists. They were people who knew deeply what God is like and what God requires from us.'

'They have never struck me as being very attractive people.'

'Then learn more about them, and think again. And remember that in the Writings, books like Job and the Psalms and Proverbs, we find a third form of ethical teaching. There

What To Do?

one is told to listen to Wisdom, especially as taught by the older men, and never to give way to its opposite, folly. "The fear of the Lord is the beginning of wisdom," and when one learns it, things will go much better. "Do the wise thing, the good thing, and you will prosper" is a kind of glorified common sense.'

'But that isn't common sense. Everyone knows that good people don't always prosper and that rogues sometimes do.'

'True, and that remains a special sort of mystery with these writers, as with the prophets, and as with us. They wonder why the righteous get knocked down and end up in the bottom of the pile. So the book of Job sits there in the middle of these Writings as a sort of question mark, asking why the righteous life doesn't always work out nicely.'

'Then perhaps I fancy the prophets best of the three.'

'It isn't a matter of who or what one likes best. We need to listen to all three forms. There is a place in everyone's life for laws and rules. There is a place for doing the wise thing, in fear of God. And there is a place for asking, "Is this appropriate for the sort of God who is calling me?", as the prophets do. To get the flavour of all this, read some of the key passages. Start with Deuteronomy 24 26, and notice the range of situations that is covered. But there is special concern for the poor. And it is a male-centred society. Then get the feel of the prophets. Read Isaiah 1, with its passion for justice and hatred of hypocrisy. Notice Jeremiah 22 and see how kings too must serve God and be corrected. Finally, look in the wisdom books at Proverbs 6 and Psalm 24.1–6, where simply and straightforwardly the qualities of the good person are sketched out. Ask yourself at the end, "Doesn't God speak to me too in such ways?" That is the key question, for both Jew and Christian.'

'But by dipping in like that we ignore huge swathes of teaching.'

'Quite right too. There are many passages about the sacrificial system, now rendered obsolete by Christ. Much of the agricultural law, not to mention the details of what foods to eat, is also out of date. Moreover, nobody dreams now, thank God, of putting to death women who commit adultery or homosexuals. And many regulations have been ignored for centuries: for example, the prohibition of usury – that is, taking interest on loans – would make the modern financial system collapse overnight! We see all these regulations as belonging only to a past culture, a past form of worship, a past stage in the human story. God has moved on, and we must move on too.'

'So we can't avoid being selective. I must come to terms with that.'

Questions for discussion

1. What value do you see in the Old Testament teachings on ethics?

2. On what basis should we distinguish acceptable from unacceptable biblical teaching?

12

Ethics in the New Testament

Matthew's teacher began by asking, 'What do you know about the New Testament and the ethics discussed there?', and Matthew replied, 'I know that the New Testament teaches that God is love, and that we have to be loving too, following Jesus.'

The teacher was unimpressed. 'As a matter of fact, "God is love" only occurs once, because the main concern in the New Testament is with the character of God's love and the kind of love that is required from us. We see it in Jesus, who is the final word about God's loving. In him we discern that God's love is indiscriminate, passionate, active, sacrificial, incredibly generous, forgiving, and offered as sheer grace because we could never possibly deserve it.'

'But I'm right about Jesus teaching the way of love, surely?'

'Of course. But his teaching is all by way of challenge and encouragement to live, as he put it, "in the Kingdom". Such a way of life combines a wholehearted love of God and a willingness to love our neighbour as ourselves. It is, in short, a response to the two great commandments, the key to life as God wants it to be. As Jesus talks about it, one senses that the best of the Old Testament teaching has been gathered together and then taken much further.'

'But what of the three forms you told me to read and study?'

'Jesus doesn't scorn the commandments but develops them. He wants us to capture the intention behind them rather than their letter, and never to imagine that keeping them earns God's approval for us. He points out that sometimes one can't keep one without breaking another, and that therefore discernment is needed. Again, Jesus speaks like a prophet. A passage like Matthew 5.43–48 is wholly prophetic in style: "Be perfect in the same way that God is." And he values wisdom – "Be wise as serpents and harmless as doves" (Matthew 10.16) – whilst the vivid little story of the two houses is classic wisdom teaching (Matthew 7.24–27). In fact, the Sermon on the Mount (Matthew 5–7) is an invaluable collection of Jesus' teaching, plus encouragement in prayer.'

'I thought that Jesus was meant to be the most original ethical teacher ever?'

'Like all good teachers, he didn't offer something totally new but built on the past. What was so startling about Jesus was the way he saw the truth, the way he put it over, the way he lived it out. He practised what he preached – total trust in God, total love for God, no matter what it cost; and he died forgiving those who crucified him. He never gave way to hatred or violence. Christians can't help seeing in him the Ideal Man.'

'What about Paul? I get the impression that his teaching was heavy going, and nothing like as plain as Jesus'. Besides, he seemed to have had a down on women, and told them to keep quiet.'

'You have probably never read his letters carefully. The first feature is that he doesn't appear to have heard of Jesus' teaching. He uses a different style and vocabulary, but is actually teaching something very similar. He says that with Jesus' coming there is a new state of affairs altogether. Trusting God means being put right by him. We can put away the old, weak things and can begin on a new way altogether, leading into satisfying, loving, exciting life with Jesus. The Holy Spirit – which means Jesus with us – will be encouraging us into all that is good and new and loving. Read Galatians 5.13–26 and then try Colossians 3.1–17. Such passages give us the form of the teaching.'

'But lots of Christians say that Paul is old-fashioned.'

'In some ways he is. He often writes, not surprisingly, like a typically first-century person. He reckons that men should rule over women. He seems to see nothing wrong in slavery. He thinks homosexuality is like idolatry. He even says that women should wear hats in church to stop angels getting into their hair and causing trouble! He appears to give unqualified support to the Roman authorities. But all that wasn't the core of his teaching, where he says over and over again, "Let the Spirit of Christ lead you, so that you grow in the ways of love."'

'So he is old-fashioned, but spells out the good news about Jesus with wonderful clarity, and that's why we listen to him? All right, but what about the other New Testament leaders and writers?'

'The same applies. Like Paul, they are people of their time and place. But they were gripped in the same way by Christ as they faced different issues. They had to write about the new needs of the young church, the leadership qualities required and the discipline, and how to face up to persecution. They were involved in a huge task of thinking, from the standpoint of faith, about God, about Jesus, about the good life, about the Jews and about the many religions of the Roman Empire. Sometimes they sound a bit ordinary, but more often they seem inspired, trying out new thoughts and ideas, with Jesus as the focal point for everything. Take a look at Titus 2 and I John 3. You'll soon see what I mean.'

'I sense that you don't see the New Testament as spelling out one set of ethical rules or teaching, but as offering a variety of ideas with some major themes – like starting a new life "in Christ" and seeing love as the supreme virtue – always at the core. Is that right?'

'Yes, and in the process we can honestly face the fact that there are some passages, rarely read in church, which nobody today treats as direct commands from God – the letter of Jude, for example, with its violent tone, or the argument in Hebrews 6 that baptized persons who lapse from the faith can never be restored again, or the naïve assertion that the love of money is the root of all evil (I Timothy 6.1) or the apparently callous judgment that those who do not work cannot eat (II Thessalonians 3.10). And, as we have seen, there is no repudiation of slavery, and few signs that the subjugation of women should be challenged.'

Matthew was quiet. 'We have to have our wits about us,' he said. 'My whole project is more complex than I had dreamed at first. It raises issues I had never thought of before. It has been marvellous for me to have to wrestle with all this. I will come back with more questions.'

Questions for discussion

1. In what ways were Jesus' teachings familiar, and to what extent new?

2. If Paul and other writers were children of their time, how should we regard them: as infallible, as inspired but limited, as interesting but irrelevant now, or in other ways?

13

Sunday Lunch

Sunday lunch was always enjoyable for the whole family. It was the one meal when they were usually all together and with plenty of time. Mother made sure that it was a good meal, and the custom had grown up that everyone helped to prepare it, serve it and clear it away. Family banter flowed freely, and often a vigorous discussion developed about the service they had just attended. If the sermon had been controversial, lunchtime saw it picked over, despite the constant complaints of Joy, the youngest, who was still in the Junior Church. And this is precisely what happened on the Sunday after Matthew had returned, constantly brooding about his project, from the last tutorial with his teacher.

The preacher had begun by saying that he didn't like some of the recent translations of his text, and that therefore he had chosen the *Good News Bible* version, which reads: 'Remember the Lord in everything you do and he will show you the right way' (Proverbs 3.6). He then explained that the *New English Bible*'s 'Think of him in all your ways and he will smooth your path' is not adequate. 'God doesn't only make your path a bit smoother,' he said. 'God shows you what your path should be.'

He had given three illustrations of God directing faithful people to the right path. The first arose from his experience as a community nurse. He had been called out one night to an urgent case in the countryside. The house was remote, the directions sketchy – and he hadn't visited the area before. He came to a junction where five lanes met, and felt totally lost. He prayed urgently, and some strong hunch urged him down one of the lanes. Shortly afterwards he realized that the house he wanted was in front of him. He brought vital medical help to the patient there. God had guided him.

Then he described how his wife had been saving up for a new knitting machine. She found one advertised in a mail order

Sunday Lunch

catalogue at a bargain price. It looked ideal, but before sending off the cheque she hesitated. Something, almost a voice, seemed to be warning her, and she didn't post her order. Then last week there had been a television programme exposing that firm as a fraud. 'There you are,' said the preacher. 'God shows us the right way.'

Finally, he told about his friend, a devout Christian who suddenly found that his firm was bought out and everyone in the office was redundant. He went to the Job Centre and was told that he was too old to fill an existing post or to be retrained. He was immensely depressed and prayed earnestly about it. Then he pocketed his pride and went to four offices like his original one, only to be turned away. He almost gave up, but something urged him to try at the far end of town. When he presented himself at an office there, the manager almost fell on his neck, saying that they were desperate to get an older, experienced man and offering him a job there and then. 'Now,' said the preacher, 'he finds this job better than his previous one. God guides us into the right way.'

Matthew was very critical of the way the preacher chose his text. 'It isn't right,' he said, 'to compare all the different translations and pick the one that suits your fancy.' But the others were not so irate. 'There are many passages that say almost exactly what the preacher said,' his mother commented, 'so it didn't matter all that much.' But the illustrations were more debatable. 'Our cousin Jan prayed for guidance when she left college and wanted a child care job, and she thought that the place she chose would be fine. But look how miserable she is now. Those children are awful, and the parents are horrid to her, even though they claim to be religious.' 'I can think of Christians who have been tricked by some scam or other. Faith isn't a security system against being conned, is it?' 'What about all those unemployed Christians who have done all they possibly can and still can't get a job? Has God stopped bothering about them, or are they secretly special sinners?'

What To Do?

Father had been quiet as all these comments swirled around. Finally, Matthew said to him, 'What do you think, Dad? I suppose that, as an engineer, you look for other explanations of all that the preacher said?'

'I know that there are problems with those examples,' his father replied, 'but there is still something in what the preacher was trying to say. God is always trying to guide us into right ways and sometimes, when we are sincerely seeking guidance, we can sense a pressure pushing us in a certain direction. I am sure, indeed, that most Christians would agree about this. The experience may not be spectacular, but it is real nevertheless.'

'Then why doesn't it happen for every puzzled believer all the time?' asked Matthew. 'It would be mighty helpful if it did.'

'Partly because we are reluctant to be really receptive,' said Mother. 'It's hard to be saying to God, "Send me wherever you want", and to be open to every good possibility. We tend to lay down too many conditions, like, "Send me anywhere so long as I am well paid", and that sort of thing. And that shields us from God.'

Joy piped up with charming simplicity. 'Melanie asked God to heal her mother. But he didn't. So she's become an atheist. What's an "atheist"?' Everyone laughed and proffered definitions. Joy went on, 'But why, if God is meant to lead us in the right path, didn't God answer her prayer? Did he want her Mum to die and leave all that family to manage on their own?'

Mother replied, 'We just don't know why. It's the everlasting mystery I live with almost every day. Sometimes we get a patient, a dedicated Christian, who has lots of people praying for them, and they make a surprising recovery. They praise God and reckon that their restored life is a miracle. But other patients in similar circumstances don't recover. When they die, sometimes slowly and painfully, everyone feels let down by

Sunday Lunch

God and baffled. We simply have to accept that that's the way it is.'

Matthew said, 'But that's not quite what the preacher was saying. He didn't talk about sickness and healing. He said we would be guided if we had a moral problem or a crucial choice to make. I don't think that everyone I've interviewed would see it like that. Many would feel that it makes Christian living sound too easy. "Come to Jesus", and no problems afterwards.'

'Be fair,' said his Father. 'The preacher never said that. He confessed that sometimes we have to struggle hard for guidance, and it may take ages, or be the opposite of what we want. One has to be totally open, as Mum says. But it may come through the way things transpire. I hear that Jan has had another offer and can leave that first family. Maybe her first experience, wretched though it has been, has been good for her in all sorts of ways, and the new post may turn out to be happy. Looking back, she may feel that she has been guided all along.'

'But you appear to be saying that, whatever happens, Jan has been guided,' said Matthew. 'And that seems like wanting to have your cake and eat it. Any critic of your line can't win. God is always guiding us, even if we have to go through hell. What kind of God would make Jan have a terrible time with those beastly people?'

'That's not quite how I view it,' said Father. 'I see God always nudging us towards what is good, even though we live in a rough and tumble and sinful world in which we meet with downs as well as ups, sorrows as well as joys. Maybe he nudged Jan into the first job because it was better than nothing, and on to the new one because it is better still, and so on. And he is always wanting us to grow, whatever situation we are put in. Grow to be a better person, he says, even though you are by no means in heaven yet.'

'But why say that he nudges us? The preacher put it much more strongly than that.'

What To Do?

'Well, I have reservations about his line. I think that God is always trying to attract us towards what is good, whether we pray about it or not. But he never forces us, never shouts at us. It is much more subtle than that, just as the force of gravity, quietly and invisibly, is always drawing us in a certain way. We get so used to it that we rarely think about it, but it helps keep the whole universe together.'

'I like that,' said Matthew. 'And the idea of gravity is better than that of God nudging us. If you get nudged, you can't help feeling it. But gravity goes on unnoticed.'

'Then perhaps we should use both ideas,' said Mother. 'For I think that there are unusual times when we get a nudge, or even a kick, from God. Clear indications are given, and we shouldn't rule them out altogether. People do hear something, almost like a voice calling to them. But it's easy to be deceived; and, though not dismissing such indications out of hand, we have to test them,'

Carol, now fifteen and anxious to be as involved as possible, interjected, 'What about that preacher a few weeks ago who said that we should "put out a fleece", or some such phrase, and that would be the test? She said that she once put two bits of paper into a hat, one saying "Yes" and the other "No". Having prayed a lot and drawn out the one that said "No", she ditched her boy friend. Then, later, she repeated the process with another boyfriend and, having drawn out "Yes", married him.'

'Oh, she was a bit barmy,' said Matthew. 'And I hope I never go steady with someone as daft as that.' 'Me too,' said Carol feelingly.

Questions for discussion

1. Have you ever had experiences like those described by the preacher? Do they stand up to the criticisms voiced here?

Sunday Lunch

2. How wary should we be of special 'hunches'? What tests should we apply to them?

3. Is God's influence like the attractive power of gravity? Can you think of better ways of picturing God's care for us?

4. Is God likely to use the casting of lots as a good way of showing us his will? What is helpful and unhelpful about that method?

Part 2

Thinking Through the Issues

14

Do Your Own Thing?

Everyone, according to Matthew's journalist uncle, must choose their own standards, since there are no values built into the universe which are binding on human beings as such. The suggestion is that it is part of our freedom as persons to decide not only what career to follow but also what moral values to live by. And, as Matthew discovered, the idea produces plenty of comment.

It seems at first sight as if it must be true. Look at the great differences between the major religions and the ways they encourage their believers to behave. Buddhists are taught to respect every possible form of life, from the beetle to the human being. But members of other faiths will squash an obtrusive beetle with no compunction whatever. Though strict Muslims insist that women be veiled in public, other faiths have no such requirement. Similarly, though Sikhs must wear turbans, Christians can sport any headgear or none. And so we could go on. Moral obligations seem to vary enormously between religions.

There is variety too within the life of a single nation. In England, for example, the well-to-do regard shop-lifting as outrageous, while the poor don't. Young people reckon that loud, late-night parties are great fun, whereas older folk are appalled by them. Some groups tolerate the use of cannabis, others are furiously opposed, and the political parties differ.

Perhaps most strikingly of all, Christians differ greatly amongst themselves. The Catholic Church is wholly opposed to all abortion and contraception, while most other Christians aren't. Some Methodists advocate teetotalism and are appalled by all gambling, whereas most other Christians aren't. Some Christians are pacifists, but the majority aren't. It all seems to be a matter of preference or taste. It doesn't look as if everyone in the world, or even everyone who is a Christian, sees specific

What To Do?

moral obligations as universally binding. Instead, we select what shall count as our duties, and are greatly influenced by our class or nation or religion as we do so. We are reluctant, moreover, ever to say that our choice is 'right', lest we sound arrogant.

Then consider the great popularity of what is termed 'counselling'. For some time, it has been customary to advise those who are worried or have experienced some trauma or are finding it hard to cope with life to see a counsellor, who will help them to look inside themselves at what they really feel, and then at what they really want. Counsellors must not in any circumstances appear judgmental or suggest their own scale of values, since for 'clients' the road to mental – and presumably moral – health is to be helped to grasp their real desires and to pursue them. This approach has undoubtedly been of huge assistance to many troubled people, but it quietly assumes that questions of truth and moral adequacy (e.g., Is this desire of mine truly directed towards the full life?) should never be asked.

There are, in fact, serious flaws in the whole approach. First of all, it isn't true to our experience of moral obligation. A person caught up in an acute moral dilemma, far from believing that he or she can choose what values are to matter, always feels that there are some things that one must do, no matter what the cost. If, for example, one sees a big boy bullying a small one, one feels a surge of rage. That's wrong! One doesn't pause and contemplate the different scales of values that boys might hold to or have been brought up with. One wants to stop it, and is troubled until the offending behaviour has been put right. The offence is felt to be against the 'law of life' rather than against some personal values of one's own choosing.

Secondly, moral relativism is itself a curiously dogmatic position. It lays down the law that everyone must choose values for themselves, must never pretend that their values are better than other people's, and must be tolerant of all other standards.

Do Your Own Thing?

This position isn't, of course, one that can be proved, but its take-it-or-leave-it feel leads to a further comment: it contrasts starkly with the way that science proceeds. Suppose two research physicists are trying to find out how fast light travels through a liquid. One gets a result which is twice the other's. Each researcher doesn't then say, 'Oh well, let's not be intolerant about this. Let both results stand.' Rather, each of them will check back time and time again, repeating the experiments until they are agreed on the figure. They will assume, in other words, that in such circumstances the pursuit of truth is more important than tolerance.

But there are further flaws. If everyone chooses their own moral positions and principles, human community is profoundly weakened. Suppose in a family each of the five members says, 'I don't like the food you others fancy. I will only eat what I feel like eating today. I will cook my own and eat it on my own. It's part of my essential freedom as a human being.' Then the community which accompanies a shared meal, even if there are disagreements whilst it proceeds, is lost. An important social glue has been removed, and human togetherness has been undermined. No community, in fact, can possibly continue if every member is free to choose which laws they will observe and which they will scorn. No state can cope with people who demand the right to drive either on the right or left as suits their whim or, more seriously, to pay only the tax they themselves have decided is legitimate and affordable.

We turn next to a particularly deep flaw. Moral relativism carries the implicit assumption that everyone chooses sensible and helpful values to live by. But human nature isn't like that, and not to notice its dark side is to be astonishingly naïve! Thus if someone most desires to be a paedophile, it would be wrong to counsel them on how best to find that sort of fulfilment; and if someone else most desires to commit rape, it would be irresponsible to say, 'Oh very well, you are free to choose what values you wish.' In both cases, there is a profound moral duty

What To Do?

to try to direct them away from such practices, which will harm others and themselves. In short, there is general agreement that such actions are WRONG, whether their intending perpetrators think so or not.

A further reflection. After the Second World War, there was a general longing for a better world and the United Nations, a body which tried to lay down rules for international behaviour, was formed. The UN promoted the Universal Declaration of Human Rights and invited all nations to subscribe to it. This Declaration asserts that a whole string of 'rights' belong inherently to human beings by virtue of their humanity.

Such Human Rights have acquired immense importance since 1949. They are constantly quoted in politics and law, and it is slowly becoming a mark of a 'good' nation that it expresses these rights adequately in its own laws and tries to encourage all other governments to honour them. There is little deep discussion, however, of how these presumed rights actually occur, or whence they originate, or why we say that everyone has them. If those questions are pushed hard, Christians have to say, 'Why, they are given us by God, who creates us with this inherent dignity.' But the moral relativist has no conceivable answer to offer. For if everyone chooses their own values, no one is obliged to recognize the 'rights' of anyone else. The strong support for human rights, therefore, now seen to be utterly essential for all humanity, is undermined if the illusion of moral relativism is maintained.

But we are still left with the great differences between the moral teachings of the different faiths and even the different Christian traditions. If there are some absolute moral obligations which we all must honour, whatever our faith or worldview, how can there be such divergences amongst the faithful? Here it is helpful to discriminate between what one may term 'first order' principles and 'second order' ones. The former are those which Christians believe to be basic, like the 'fruit of the Spirit' in the New Testament.

Do Your Own Thing?

The second order are more concerned with how the first are actually applied. Do they imply the refusal to use violence against other human beings – and therefore, perhaps, pacifism? Does the foetus in the womb qualify as a human being or not – a key issue in the abortion debate? Which obligation is to be preferred when different duties conflict with each other – for example, should a mother steal food for her starving children? Should a repentant sex offender be fully welcomed back into normal society and maybe into the company of children? Should we permit divorce?

Those second order principles require judgment, wisdom, the weighing up of various options, and knowledge of how previous generations have coped. But these qualities are not infallibly present in any church or any individual Christian. Therefore it is inevitable that there will be differences at this point. It is as if God says to us, 'I give you the great fundamental principles as plainly as can be and especially in the person of Jesus. But you must use your own wits to discern how they should work out in all the ups and downs of normal life. If you differ about that, keep talking with each other and listening to each other as you seek my will. Don't be cross with each other and don't be aggressive, but hold to Christ.'

Questions for discussion

1. Is moral relativism, despite is weaknesses, preferable to hardline and dogmatic religious teaching?

2. What actions or intentions can we describe as always wrong?

3. How would you justify the differences between Christians on such a vital matter as killing in war?

What To Do?

4. If morals are not relative, what should be taught in the home, in the school, in the church?

5. Some preachers and commentators imply that moral standards today are declining. Can you point to signs of decline, and of improvement?

6. Although human rights are not directly cited in the Bible, how should Christians view them?

15

How Not To Use The Bible

Some Christians regard the Bible as a compendium of moral instruction, something like a car manual covering every situation which a motorist is likely to encounter. The car won't start? Turn to page 7 in the Manual and follow the advice you find there. The car will probably start but, if not, ring the garage! Similarly, some Christians believe that, when there is a problem, the Bible will somewhere provide relevant help. This was certainly the conviction of the young Youth Fellowship helper. When faced with the question of which local church to attend, he looked to scripture for assistance. The Bible, on this view, is a massive encyclopaedia of God's answers to our ethical problems.

The approach sometimes reassures those who use it. Matthew, of course, wasn't at all persuaded of its value, and even regarded one such Christian as 'barmy'. But the person concerned probably felt confident of God's guidance. So what's wrong with the approach? Well, to begin with, there are a host of profound problems which are never mentioned in the Bible because they have emerged since. What level of risk is acceptable in the generation of nuclear power? What political party should I support? Should I join a union? Should we permit euthanasia? What about the use of cannabis? Condoms? Cloning?

Moreover, as the teacher pointed out, the Bible contains plenty of instruction which is outdated – about operating the sacrificial system, running a farm in ancient Israel, knowing what foods to eat and clothing to wear. Most importantly, however, this moral textbook approach distorts what the Bible is. As the record of humanity's crucial encounter with God, the Bible isn't primarily concerned with morality. It makes clear, rather, how openness to God is of first importance.

What To Do?

We can therefore make a simple rule: *Don't turn the Bible into a moral textbook on every conceivable problem.* To do so both distorts and dishonours scripture

The teacher began by warning Matthew about some of the teaching in the Bible. One can find many passages in the earlier parts of the Old Testament which command genocide and countenance sheer brutality. 'Every right-thinking person should recoil from it,' he said; and he was quite right. As the teacher also pointed out, we don't now put to death women who commit adultery or homosexuals; and it would be dreadful if we ever dreamed of doing so. Nor do we implement the ban on usury (interest), which would cause the financial systems to collapse at once.

It isn't difficult, either, to think of dreadful episodes in history which have been inspired by biblical teaching. The Spanish conquest of South America, justified in its time by scripture, was incredibly savage. So too was the oppression by the Boers of the native Bantu peoples in South Africa. And so we could go on. The blunt truth is that a naïve attitude towards biblical teaching, especially in its earliest forms, has caused terrible harm. We want no more of it.

How then do we discriminate between what is acceptable and what is not? As many people said to Matthew, one has to 'pick and choose', and that too can be dangerous, since there will be a temptation to choose what one fancies. Here we use the test which rings true to Paul's deepest convictions – that, difficult though it may be, we must strain every nerve to rise above our own prejudices and have 'the mind that was in Christ'. Jesus repudiated much of that Old Testament harshness. 'They were told ... but I tell you' runs through much of Matthew 5 (the opening sections of the Sermon on the Mount). For example, you used to be ordered to hate your enemies, but not so any longer. Christ, then, stands in judgment upon all savagery, including that which used to be done in God's name.

How Not To Use The Bible

We can put together another simple rule: *Don't accept biblical teaching that doesn't reflect the mind of Christ.* Instead, look to Christ, who is the judge of scripture as well as the judge of all of us. It is in Christ that we truly meet God.

One of the perils of treating the Bible as a 'Great Handbook on Moral Matters' is that we are then tempted to take an instruction from the past and transfer it into today's very different culture as if the intervening centuries hadn't happened. We cannot, as we have seen, do that with usury, and the same applies to almost any other detailed directive. Matthew tackled his mother about the relation between his aunt being a Local Preacher and Paul's ruling that women should keep quiet in church, and she replied that Paul was 'a bit old-fashioned'. A less dismissive reply would have been: 'Paul was a man of his time and culture. His judgment may well have been appropriate then, but it no longer applies in today's very different society.'

It is inappropriate, similarly, to transfer unchanged medical practice across the centuries, and we wouldn't dream of doing so. Thus we wouldn't deal with anyone suffering from an unsightly skin disease as happened in New Testament times. Instead of banning them from normal society, we would treat them with sophisticated drugs. Again, it is foolish to transfer scientific ideas across the centuries. The earth isn't, after all, a huge plate, from whose edge those venturing too far can fall. And the same applies to advice offered about the law or business or agriculture – not to mention morality. If, for example, every young man was advised to set his sights on a wife like the one described in Proverbs 31, the marriage rate amongst Christians would plummet at once!

This isn't a counsel of despair. It doesn't mean that the Bible is of no use to us as we wrestle with moral problems and priorities. It simply means that the true value of the Bible doesn't lie in providing us with handy little rules, but in opening us up to God, to truth, to the source of all that is

What To Do?

valuable, desirable and beautiful. The Bible gives us visions and ideals, not precise guidance for the problems we need to solve.

We need to put that into another rule of thumb. *Don't transfer moral teaching directly from a far-off biblical culture to today.* It simply may not fit.

Nevertheless, we all know that Christians need the Bible desperately. We need the graphic and compelling stories which spell out God's character and activity. We need the excitement, challenge and power of discovering that he is totally involved in this world and totally committed to all who live in it. We need Jesus Christ and all that the New Testament records about him as the heart-beat of our faith. And the immense range of moral insight that flows through scripture is especially helpful. As we are reminded of what Christ taught and did and of its moral implications, he becomes real to us. But is the moral insight always captured in a commandment, a sentence or two or a set of tidy rules? Generally speaking, no. The insight is to be culled from the wide stream of the Bible's witness, not from each little drop of water within it.

It follows that we are bound to be wary of taking up a particular moral matter, finding one text that refers to it, saying in a loud voice, 'The Bible says ...' and presuming that the matter is now settled. That is a lazy way of trying to gain moral insight. It obscures the fact that the Bible contains history, legend, prayer, drama, poetry, law, visions, preaching and reflection, and that each of these various forms will offer insight in its own way. A poem, after all, is different from a tragic story, and a prayer from a law.

Let's look at divorce, an example of a very important moral matter. It isn't surprising that three strands of Old Testament material look at it in quite different ways. In Deuteronomy 24.1 the Law states bluntly that a man may divorce a wife if 'he finds something objectionable in her'. But to the Prophets God's covenant with his people is like a marriage covenant, and just as he will never go back on it, neither should the Jews where their marriages are concerned. 'I hate divorce', says the prophet (Malachi 2.16), speaking in God's name. But in the Wisdom literature the subject is hardly ever mentioned. Instead there is scorn and derision for the man who lets an adulterous woman seduce him. What an utter fool he is! (see Proverbs 7).

If one goes to the New Testament the situation isn't much clearer. Jesus seems in Mark 10.9 categorically to outlaw all divorce: 'What God has joined together, let no one separate.' Yet the parallel accounts in the other Gospels put the matter differently. In Matthew 5.32 the saying has become: 'Whoever divorces his wife, except on the ground of unchastity, causes her to commit adultery ...' Here there is an exception which profoundly alters the whole issue. Divorce is permissible in one specific case – adultery by a wife. But all the instances so far are those in which the man divorces the woman in what, unlike today, was a male-centred world. To complicate matters further, Paul doesn't seem to know much about Jesus' teaching and counsels those who are married not to divorce partners who are unbelievers unless they must, at the same time allowing both wives and husbands the right to initiate divorce (I Corinthians 7.15).

To take up any of these diverse statements, then, and say 'The Bible teaches ...' would inevitably mislead one's hearers. There is no plain, clear teaching about divorce in the Bible, even though the Mark 10 statement is included firmly within the marriage service. The writers of the Bible didn't have one attitude to the subject but several, and we can't be absolutely sure of Jesus' teaching. Some scholars claim that the Mark 10 version must be the authentic saying, but a case can also be made for the Matthew version with its exception clause.

This gives us a fourth simple rule: *Don't cite only one text or passage and claim that it is 'the biblical teaching'.* There may be a host of other references to be noted and many other matters to be taken into consideration.

What To Do?

We have ended up with four negative rules:

1. Don't turn the Bible into a moral textbook on every conceivable problem.
2. Don't accept biblical teaching that doesn't reflect the mind of Christ.
3. Don't transfer moral teaching directly from a far-off biblical culture to today.
4. Don't cite only one text or passage and claim that it is 'the biblical teaching'.

If these rules had been observed by everyone in Matthew's enquiries, he would have been greatly helped.

But we need to be more positive.

Questions for discussion

1. Does the Old Testament teaching about life and worship in primitive Israel have continuing moral importance? If so, what is it?

2. In what ways can the examples of the great figures in the Bible be of moral help to us today?

3. In what ways is the New Testament an advance on the Old in its moral teachings and insights?

4. Would you wish to add any negative rules to the four listed above? If so, what?

16

The Bible – A Better Way

The previous chapter may have seemed rather negative. Can we outline a more positive way of coming to the Bible, with all our moral problems and perplexities, and finding that God speaks to us and both guides and encourages? Undoubtedly many of the people Matthew spoke to drew much help from the scriptures; and, although they may well have skipped over some of the principles outlined in the last chapter, they were good and keen people, wanting to serve God faithfully. Some of the help which they obtained, of course, took the form of feeling that God was strengthening them rather than saying to them, 'This is the way; now walk in it.' As the minister said, referring to his decision to cancel his planned marriage, 'Somehow the Bible gave me courage.'

First of all, then, we should delight in the variety in the Bible, and rejoice to find in it a source of strength. We should be profoundly thankful that it doesn't consist of books which are all of the same kind, offering exactly the same types of insight. After all, we are very different people and can be motivated in quite different ways. What stirs some people leaves others cold. Some of us don't like profound stories, like that of Jonah, unless they are literally true. Others rejoice in them. Some like pithy sayings, like those in the book of Proverbs: 'The getting of treasures by a lying tongue is a fleeting vapour and a snare of death' (Proverbs 21.6). Others find that facile. Some are stirred by the gripping visions of the good time God will bring about, when 'the wolf will live with the lamb, the leopard will lie down with the kid' (Isaiah 11.6). Others find them fanciful.

Some people can most easily grasp simple directions, as the police sergeant showed by his deep respect for the ninth commandment. Maybe that was because he lived, more than most of us, in the world of the law. Others need the fiery messages of the prophets or the powerful impact of Jesus'

What To Do?

words and actions. Matthew's mother, you will recall, acknowledged that she can't forget Jesus and doesn't want to – such is the challenge and inspiration towards the good life which he provides. And some derive help from the later New Testament books, which reveal a young church trying to be faithful to Jesus as it copes with everyday life in a turbulent empire. The police sergeant, again, was uplifted by the insights in I Peter that encourage us to promote good order in a rough world. Others, however, would find that too conservative.

Bearing all this in mind, we can offer another simple rule: *Recognizing the diverse visions and insights in the Bible, try to draw help from the full range of its styles and forms.*

Next, we have already noticed the difference between what were termed 'first order principles' and those more detailed rules or insights which help put them into practice, the 'second order principles'. If we know that God makes us special but different (first order principle), we conclude that racism is a sin, as is snobbery or blind national pride (second order principles). If it be a clear revelation from God that he values all the creatures he has made and that therefore every creature deserves equal respect (first order principle), then it must follow, as Peter discovered with the help of a vision, that Jewish Christians need not hesitate to visit Gentile Christians or treat them as equals (second order principle, Acts 10.34ff.).

This distinction is invaluable when reading the Bible. For, though the first order principles, usually underlining something vital about God, remain the same, the second order principles alter with changes in the society to which they are being applied. We need not worry, then, if we find some of the second order principles frankly ridiculous today. There are rules, for example, about what provision must be made for someone who has accidentally killed another – there must be three cities of 'refuge' to which he may flee and then be safe. Nobody seriously suggests that we must provide such cities today. Though ordered in Deuteronomy 19, such provision is a

The Bible – A Better Way

second order matter. Somewhere behind it stands a conviction that God is both just and merciful. Whereas, then, the directive itself can be abandoned without any worry whatsoever, the beliefs behind it can't.

Another way of regarding 'first order principles' is that suggested in the previous chapter. Paul says, 'Have the mind that was in Christ.' This is a very Christian way of saying, 'Look to first order principles.'

Though the first/second order distinction is a great help when reading the Bible, it isn't, alas, a perfect remedy for all our problems, for we may differ about what are first order principles and what aren't. First order principles point to God's character, to the way he handles the world and to the heart of Jesus' teaching. But is the conviction that runs right through the Bible that the male somehow reflects God more than the female a first order principle or not? If it is, as many assert, then women should be subordinate to men and should never become priests. If it isn't, as many today believe passionately, then that arrangement can be regarded as perhaps appropriate to past societies but not to today's. There's no easy way of sorting out that argument, and the Bible itself doesn't help very much in separating what can be seen as passing and what can't. So this distinction between first and second order principles – the permanent insight and the passing one, or the mind of Christ and the mind of human beings – doesn't solve every problem.

Recognizing its limitations, we offer a second rule: *Look especially for the first order principles, which usually refer to God's character and reflect the mind of Christ*. Let the second order principles be seen as transient and often no longer incumbent upon us.

Now let us take that theme further. What has been termed the 'first order principle' should be what we most encourage amongst us, what we most talk about, what we see to be the key to issue after issue, problem after problem. There were frequent hints about this in Matthew's conversations. As the businessman remarked, there are constant warnings about riches in the New Testament. One cannot escape them. Riches all too easily become a rival God, but (first order conviction) there can only be one God whom we must serve. Jesus comments clearly on this (Matthew 6.24). Therefore that insight must control all our morality. The minister commented that we can't escape hearing about our obligations to the poor, since they are 'part of the air we breathe'. It's a first order principle, of course, that God is especially the God of the poor. Eric, the young scientist, believed that we are under Christian obligation to be over-generous. Behind this lay the passionate teaching of Paul that 'God loves a cheerful giver' and is incredibly generous (first order matter). So generosity too must be part of the air we breathe, for it is integral to the witness of the Bible to God.

The young mother believed that 'love' was the key theme of the Bible, and tried to practise it in every aspect of her life. She saw it, then, as a first order matter. The application of love to different situations she recognized as more debatable, and nobody would quarrel with that. As we shall see later, her understanding of Christian morality may have been over-simplified, but she had grasped something quite essential at the heart of it. She wanted teaching about love, and the inspirational power of love, to dominate her personal life, her church and her home.

We have reached a third rule, following from the previous one: *Let first order principles dominate*, as they dominate the Bible. Thus we do indeed hear God speaking to us.

But these three rules are obviously not enough to provide the moral guidance we need, or the moral visions we desire, or the virtues we want to develop as Christians. Both the Roman Catholic doctor and the Protestant minister knew that only too well. The doctor said plainly that one can never depend on the Bible alone, not least because Christians interpret the same passages or texts very differently. The church, he therefore believed, must guide our interpretation of the Bible, for the two

The Bible – A Better Way

belong inseparably to each other. The minister was also sure that one can't go to the Bible alone to discern God's will, especially in highly problematic instances. He referred to four sources of help. Although they originated in the Church of England in Elizabeth I's day, and only later were very important to John Wesley, they have become known as the 'Wesleyan Quadrilateral'.

To sort out his moral obligations, then, the minister draws upon the Bible, the church, Christian experience, and reason. The same four sources, he could have added, help his attempts to formulate his theology, his understanding of God. The four sources together enable him to gain the necessary insights. At the same time, he would probably acknowledge, on reflection, that he would reject anything flatly contrary to the Bible's witness. The Bible, then, is a key source, but to be used in conjunction with others. It has to be read using our God-given reason, taking note of the tradition of the church and in the light of Christian experience.

Hence a fourth rule: To have an adequate view of God and insight into his will for us, *use, along with the Bible, the tradition of the church, the experience of Christians today and your own reason*. Indeed, we could probably refer back to the discussions Matthew had and discover that all four helps were operating the whole time, even if unacknowledged.

In our efforts to be more positive, then, we have discovered four more rules:

1. Recognizing the diverse visions and insights in the Bible, try to draw help from the full range of its styles and forms.
2. Look especially for the first order principles, which usually refer to God's character and reflect the mind of Christ.
3. Let first order principles dominate.
4. Use, along with the Bible, the tradition of the church, the experience of Christians today, and your own reason.

What To Do?

Questions for discussion

1. Which form of biblical literature do you find most inspiring? Poetry? Visions? History? Prayers? Preaching? Stories? Parables? Any other? Can you give reasons?

2. How useful is the distinction between what has here been termed 'first order' and 'second order' principles?

3. What do you think are the 'first order principles' as the Bible witness describes them?

4. Does the 'Wesleyan Quadrilateral' give a fair summary of the helps Christians should call on in their theology and their ethics?

17

Is Love Enough?

The young mother was quite clear about it: when Christians are puzzled about what to do they should ask the question, 'What does love require here?' She was sure that this was the plain teaching of the New Testament and that it worked best. She also knew that Jesus was the finest possible example of what that love is like. When, therefore, she and her family had to sort out the problem of the grandmother's home, this was the question they wrestled with.

Though she never used the phrase, she was advocating 'Situation Ethics', which arrived on the Christian scene in the 1960s as something of a bombshell. It was, after all, a time of radical rethinking, and all sorts of revolutionary ideas were stirring in the Christian mind. The term 'Situation Ethics' was coined by the American moralist Joseph Fletcher to describe what was called 'the only ethic for "man come of age"'. He claimed that there were really only three possibilities in the moral life – to be amoral (that is, to refuse any moral system whatever and please oneself), to follow a prescriptive code (for example, traditional Roman Catholic teaching or the ethos of old-fashioned Protestantism), or to be a 'situationist'. He wrote with great vigour and, since sexual ethics were open to reappraisal, made an immediate contribution to what was a key concern of the times.

Fletcher taught that the only consideration, when faced by a moral dilemma, was 'What does love require?' Nothing else mattered. Moreover, the love he was advocating was, he claimed, the wholly unselfish and demanding goodwill called *agape* in the New Testament and taught and demonstrated by Jesus. It was therefore unfair, he protested, for his critics to accuse him of wanting to be 'permissive'. For he wasn't arguing that one should seek happiness or self-fulfilment or gratification or ignore all normal sensibilities about right and

What To Do?

wrong. He did claim, however, that this special agape-love – which he saw as creative, imaginative and innovative – might make one override established rules, since it had to be considered afresh in every situation.

This approach is very attractive. It makes many an ethical problem much more simple. If 'What does love require?' is the all-important consideration, one doesn't need to know a whole mass of texts from the Bible, or be versed in canon law, or have a sophisticated knowledge of the roles of conscience, or intuition, or natural law, or of any of the other matters that moralists debate. The key, one is told, is to use reason to calculate how to produce the most loving outcome in every case. It is a method for plain, dedicated Christians who want to get things right and need simple but strong guidance.

Further, it's an approach which can be used in unusual situations for which there are few precedents. Seeking the right course of action in uncharted waters is always especially difficult, and Fletcher was very imaginative in citing instances. Take one of his examples. A German family was separated in the awful chaos at the end of the Second World War. The father finally found his three children, but the mother was in a Russian camp, from which the only way of release was by being pregnant. She persuaded a guard to impregnate her, got her release, and was able to be reunited with her children. Fletcher says that she did what love for the family required, all other moral factors, including the prohibition of adultery, being of less importance.

Despite the gusto with which Fletcher argued, 'situation ethics' has been sharply criticized since 1966 and hasn't won the support of many contemporary thinkers. Here are the four main criticisms levelled against it.

First, is it true that this is what the New Testament advocates or Jesus taught? The more one reads the New Testament the less convincing Fletcher's claim becomes. Scholars certainly disagree strongly about the matter. Some, for example, claim

Is Love Enough?

that, according to Jesus' teaching, one must respond to God's present actions in promoting his Kingdom and making life better. Others point out that in St Mark's Gospel Jesus never tells his disciples to love and that love isn't mentioned in the Acts of the Apostles or Hebrews or the book of Revelation. And whilst Paul does indeed teach that love fulfils the law, he doesn't wonder about the most loving thing to do when discussing many of the moral problems presented to him. It's a huge over-simplification, therefore, to narrow biblical teaching to the love command.

Second, is love as novel and unpredictable as situation ethics suggests? Is it possible, for example, to conceive a situation in which a mother, seeking the way of love, wouldn't put the feeding of her child before feeding herself? If not, one can simply say that, as a clear rule, the child's hunger comes before the mother's, That is, love is consistent, and one can therefore helpfully put together some 'rules' which show which way it will go. Moreover – to note a subsidiary point – a mother is thus saved from having to sit down each time she faces that situation and wrack her brains about what to do, for she has a rule to guide her.

The third objection concerns two aspects of human nature. Are we so attuned to the compulsions of love that whenever we are in a moral quandary we can readily know what the most loving thing is? Are we able, indeed, to calculate the results of various possible actions, and conclude with certainty, 'If I do action A, it will produce a more loving outcome than if I do action B'? To answer 'Yes' in both cases presumes, unrealistically, that the insight and wisdom of a saint can regularly be coupled with a superhuman understanding of the complexities of our world. Such an approach to ethics is for super-Christians only!

And then, fourthly, how do we know what is to be reckoned as part of the 'situation' and what is not? The advocates of situation ethics offer no direct help in this area, but the examples which they use always suggest that one should consider the persons immediately involved and nothing much else. Take, for example, one of the moral quandaries which cropped up when Matthew was talking to Julie, the scientist. She found herself aghast at the plight of the animals being used for experiments with drugs. If one were to ask, 'What is the most loving thing in this situation?', one could start by presuming that the 'situation' being discussed was that particular laboratory, its range of animals, the staff caring for them and the scientists constantly popping in and asking for this or that experiment to be conducted. In that case the most loving thing could well be to relocate all the animals in big runs, release many of them, give the staff a freer hand with them, and tell the scientists to request very few experiments in future.

But perhaps the 'situation' is bigger than that. Perhaps it involves the whole firm and all its work to relieve asthma and many other diseases. Then the 'situation' becomes many factories spread over the world, a large workforce and a board of directors somewhere or other. Or is that too small? Maybe it involves all human beings suffering from asthma and from the other diseases the firm is tackling. Or is that too small? Is the 'situation' that of all drug companies the world over, with the sort of procedures they all adopt, the pressures they work under, and the relentless public demand for cures? Or is the situation bigger still, involving the attitudes of humanity in general both to disease and to our dominion over the animals? There is no suggested way of sorting this problem out. As a result, the tendency is always for the 'situation' to be viewed on the smallest possible scale, concern being focussed on the people immediately involved.

This has unfortunate results. It means that situation ethics has never been of great help when the big social questions have had to be addressed. Can one imagine the Cabinet meeting at 10 Downing Street to decide on the next Budget, and the

Is Love Enough?

Chancellor saying, 'It's all quite easy really. We merely have to decide what is the most loving thing to do'? Equally, to consider an issue on a smaller scale, can one imagine the businessman interviewed by Matthew saying, 'When I consider my shareholders and how much of our profits we pay out as dividends to them, all I have to ask is what is the most loving thing to do'? For both Chancellor and manager there are technical issues to be addressed. The manager, for example, must work out how much profit should be ploughed back, what wage increases should be paid, and how far costs can be reduced to make the company more competitive. It's difficult to see how 'the most loving thing to do' is directly related to these matters.

The 'situationist' way of tackling a moral problem is most appropriate, perhaps, when the dilemma concerns two persons only; for example, should I marry this man or woman? But all moral problems have a nasty habit of being bigger than we first think. A question like, 'Should the two of us live together as partners without being married?' appears to be one which only concerns the two people involved. But, in fact, the answer given affects public opinion, attitudes to marriage, and thus other people's lives. No man ... or woman ... or marriage ... or partnership is an island.

Questions for discussion

1. Does the New Testament indicate that 'love' is the sole moral norm we should be guided by? If not, what other guides or norms does it suggest?

2. What situations can we think of in which 'the most loving thing to do' was clearly the major consideration we needed to resolve?

What To Do?

3. What factors should Julie have considered when pondering the morality of the work she was doing?

4. What qualities does the businessman pictured above require when sorting out his major financial concerns? Is love in any way relevant and, if so, how?

18

Be Good, As a Rule

Every child in the playground knows that good games need clear rules. Everyone learning to drive knows that absorbing and keeping the *Highway Code* is absolutely essential. Everyone running the simplest organization knows that, without basic rules, the group disintegrates into rival factions. But everyone also knows how irksome rules can be, stifling initiative and tripping us up in unexpected ways. And everyone knows how easily the nit-picking person, who has always mastered the rulebook better than everyone else, can become an authority figure to whom we all turn, asking: 'Are we permitted to do so and so, or not?'

In the ordinary run of life, then, rules are needed on all sides. But they can be a thorough nuisance. This tension – they are essential but also a threat – runs through the biblical witness, the tradition of the church, the teaching of the great moralists and, especially, the attacks made on Christian morality by thinkers far and wide. Eric, you will recall, objected that his minister 'lays down the law too much'. On the other hand, the businessman established firm rules ('Our people must always tell the truth'); the police sergeant regarded the rules governing his work as vital, even though he sometimes broke them; and Matthew, who noticed the codes of behaviour operating in many walks of life, recognized, when pressed, that on the whole they were 'a good thing'.

There is a difference between a 'rule' and a 'law'. A 'law', as befits something that should not be broken, has a feeling of absoluteness about it. Moreover, it is likely that a moral law (e.g., 'Thou shalt not steal') will be expressed in civil law too and then become a statute applying to everyone in the community. There are, of course, exceptions, A venerable moral law, 'Thou shalt not commit adultery', is not enshrined in civil law and therefore adultery is not a civil offence.

What To Do?

A 'rule', on the other hand, is not so absolute and is rarely expressed in civil law. A rule is a general guide to right, wise, appropriate behaviour. It is, for example, a widely recognized rule that, if there is a queue for some service or other, in a shop or station or office, the last person to arrive goes to the back. There is no law about it, but 'as a rule' people observe it. There are occasions when a flustered person will rush, apologetically, to the front and beg pardon from those there ('My bus is just going, please let me in first'), and that's all right. No law has been broken; rather, a rule has been shown to be flexible. Faced by acute difficulties such flexibility is quite acceptable.

The Old Testament is full of laws. Jewish scholars have always maintained, as Matthew's teacher pointed out, that there are 248 positive ones and 365 negative. But that doesn't mean that morality was seen as simply a matter of keeping them all. There are powerful appeals to 'righteousness', and later to 'wisdom', reverberating through the scriptures. In other words, it was never conceived that law could adequately express our moral obligations, and it isn't difficult to see why. It's impossible to conceive a law which would prescribe the right behaviour for every couple facing the problem of whether or not granny should come and live with them. It's equally impossible to formulate laws about how lifetime partners should be chosen. In both cases human happiness and the well-being of society can be profoundly affected and therefore the right guidance is invaluable. But laws can't tell anyone what to do and what not to do in every possible situation.

Again, laws don't describe motives and intentions, but deal with actions. A moment's thought, however, reminds us that motives are the key to good or right living. I'm plotting, let us assume, to murder an enemy, but haven't yet succeeded. I have broken no law, but I have sinned, deeply and horribly, by harbouring such evil within me. Again, I despise, let us say, all teenagers and constantly belittle their achievements. I'm a gross sinner, allowing such festering malice to corrupt my inner

Be Good, As a Rule

self and my behaviour, but I have broken no law. Law, then, indicates bad or good behaviour; it can't evaluate motive and the nature of a person's will. It's understandable that biblical teaching concentrates more upon motives, the nature of the good will and the virtues and goals we should aim at than upon our keeping laws, however admirable.

There are snags, then, with law as a means of promoting moral behaviour, and it may be helpful to list one or two more. For example, law-keeping tends to deny our creativity and spontaneity, making our obedience mechanical rather than imaginative. Again, it offers no help to us when we have to choose between rival sets of law-style obligations – e.g., what to do if one law requires me to pay a big tax bill and another to support my family, and I have little money. Once more, if morality is a matter of keeping laws, it tends to identify our actions as either good or bad, according to the law or contrary to it – whereas everyone knows that, in practice, the moral life often involves choosing between different shades of grey. I frequently, in fact, find myself opting for the lesser of two evils, or the greater of two goods, or a mixture of both.

These obvious objections aren't as telling when applied to abiding by rules, but they can't be completely disregarded. Rule-keeping, like law-keeping, focusses upon actions rather than intentions; doesn't cover the problem of how to treat granny; tends to make us mechanically obedient rather than creative; offers little help where competing obligations are concerned; and conveys little sense of the moral ambiguity of many situations. So rule-keeping, like law-keeping, can never be a satisfactory way of describing the moral life, or the Christian life. It can become, rather, an approach to life which is rooted in fear – I must not offend against any rule – rather than in a positive hunger for all that is good.

But this chapter started with noting that rules and laws are absolutely essential. We simply can't manage without them. We can't possibly live in a society which has no laws about

What To Do?

driving, or violence between persons, or truth-telling; and we wouldn't be happy about one in which, because there were no accepted rules, there were no queues but only scrums, with the weakest going to the wall. We have to have laws and rules, and in the life of the church we have to have them too. So there must be positive things to be said about law-keeping and rule-keeping, and about the need for codes of conduct in most professions, and for a Patients' Charter in the local hospital or a Users' Charter in the local railway station.

In the first place, since others in the past have faced many of the problems which beset us, rules are useful in gathering together the accumulated wisdom of the ages. Just as in every gardening society, so in medicine or law or science or business, there will be wise old hands who can offer rules, culled from vast experience, to beginners. In effect, they say: lots of experience has shown that it is better to do A rather than B so, as a rule, do A. Similarly, the Christian community can offer to its members wise counsel in the form of rules, all drawn from centuries of Christian living throughout the world, and probably stemming from convictions expressed in the Bible. So, for example, Christians can be taught to be obedient citizens, to pay their taxes, and to observe the laws of the land – unless, of course, the State requires them to act against their assured and mature conscience. For in that last resort we must 'obey God rather than man'. Such teaching, then, is more like a rule than a law because we know that there are limits to its application. It isn't a law, absolute and to be obeyed in all circumstances, but a fine rule whose wisdom has been tested and tried.

Again, rules are especially helpful to beginners, the immature, the weak, and those who need to lean heavily upon more experienced people. To those entering new territory they offer a map which shows the best route to the desired goal. We would, therefore, be failing those beginners grievously if we said to them: 'There are no rules, you just discover by trial and error what seems good.' At the same time, it must be stressed that rules, like laws, can date, and the church must constantly re-examine them.

To sum up: Christians and many others recognize the need for rules, not laws, in the moral life. Such rules are guides, not directives that permit of no exception, and they don't answer all our needs. Nor do they express the full character of Christian morality – for that we need Christian goals, virtues and visions. But they can provide a good introduction to what is moral, and general guidance for everyone, whether Christian or not, about appropriate behaviour in all walks of life.

Questions for discussion

1. What insights does the New Testament offer concerning the usefulness of law in the moral life?

2. What laws or rules in the Bible do you think apply plainly to today and to all times?

3. What moral rules, once widely accepted within the church, have had to be re-minted as a consequence of social change? Has the process of re-minting been a positive or negative experience?

4. When should Christians refuse to obey the State?

19

What Use Should the Church Be?

Imagine the following: the preacher is lamenting the worrying social trends which show how far the nation has drifted away from its Christian roots, and cites the greedy scramble for huge sums of money by company directors, footballers and pop stars, the steady rise in crime, the collapse of traditional family marriage standards, the sex and vile language on TV, the corruption in politics. These show 'a nation that has abandoned God'. Many people say afterwards what a fine sermon it was; others, mainly younger, disagree and don't want that preacher to come again.

The Christmas Fair is being planned. One committee member suggests a raffle with 50p tickets and some simple prizes. 'It will add to the fun.' Another member retorts fiercely, 'Gambling is wicked. When I was young the church had the courage to say so loud and clear. Now we want to throw away those high standards for the sake of a few paltry pounds. It's disgusting. If you agree to it I shall resign.'

The Youth Group is having an intense discussion on sexual practice. A leader says adamantly, 'The church and the Bible have always taught that adultery is sin. So is fornication. Every Christian must be chaste before marriage and faithful to the partner afterwards. That's the plain law of God.' Another leader shakes her head and says, 'It is not quite as simple as that.'

The Church Council is told that a young woman member who is unmarried has just had a baby and wants it baptized. She refuses to name the father, so he will not be present. Some members suggest that this means that it cannot be a 'Christian' baptism; others think the mother ought to be disciplined and maybe lose membership; others say that she needs the church more than ever. The Council is hopelessly divided.

What Use Should the Church Be?

The Confirmation Class has been encouraged to ask searching questions. A young man enquires about the church's teaching on war and whether or not it would support him in being a conscientious objector in wartime. One person says that her father was a pacifist in the last war and was prevented from serving as a lay preacher as a result. Someone else remarks that the church never seems to have been against any recent wars, so it must have been in favour of them. The minister seems to flounder in response.

The District Synod is debating a motion brought forward by two young members, that the age of consent for homosexual acts should be the same as for heterosexual ones, that is, sixteen. Much passion is roused by this. Some members argue furiously that the Bible teaches that homosexuality is a sin, so the motion must he rejected. Some say that 'Gays have rights, as much as anyone else.' One lone voice suggests that the real issue is the age at which anyone whatever can make responsible moral judgments, and if it is 16 for some it should be the same for all. The motion is narrowly lost after a senior figure says that there are 'more important matters for this body to be debating'.

All of these everyday examples show the church, in one forum or another, having to struggle with difficult moral problems, and not doing terribly well. Many of them show that in order to have a plain discipline (essential in any institution, let alone a church) there needs to be clear teaching carrying the weight of the church's reflection and authority. Many indicate that, if the church had any official moral teaching, the people involved did not know of it (like Matthew's mother). Others show how easy it is to bandy about phrases like 'The Bible says . . .' or to present moral issues as if they are very simple indeed, only requiring a quick law or two. But they are all slightly unfair, for the church is not always as uncertain or confused as these examples suggest.

What To Do?

So what should the church be like in order to help her members come to wise and Christian judgments, and to make a healthy moral witness to the world at large? It should, first of all, be a place where moral matters can he discussed and debated courteously, without rancour or passionate prejudice, and without all those involved being determined to be proved right. It requires a humble desire by the participants to discover together a reasonably common mind, or, failing that, to respect difference of opinion. Within the Christian community the main intention is not simply to end up with everyone in agreement, or everyone happy, or some innocuous platitudes having been bandied about – it can, for example, be presumed that everyone is 'against sin' – but to have handled diversity of approach with sufficient creativity as to have come nearer to the mind in Christ.

This means that the worship life of the church does indeed need to be inspiring, challenging, full of grace and the constant promises of God. It should focus everyone on Christ with profound regularity; this will inevitably mean that over and over again the supreme virtues of faith, hope and love are held up for all to seek and find, and the gifts of the Spirit are expected. Christian worship is not primarily designed to make us more moral, but to praise God and celebrate the gospel, which offers us new life in Christ; but an inevitable by-product is that we are caught up in that new life and begin to discover what it is like and how it can be sustained. As a sober matter of fact, the best thing the church can ever offer anyone is constant, faithful and invigorating worship.

Throughout her life the church needs to be handling the Bible responsibly. That has already been discussed in previous chapters. She also needs to present her own mature moral reflections cogently, clearly and honestly. Here most churches are not very brilliant. The members may not have the faintest idea what they are, or they may be couched in stiff technical language remote from the ordinary Christian. But most churches have been trying hard to do this, and in the process they hope that the world at large will also listen. Thus the Roman Catholic Bishops issued a fine document in 1966 entitled *The Common Good*, in which it put forward plain arguments suggesting what sort of society Christians work and pray for. It began: 'Can managers treat employees in any way they like? Is the law of the jungle the right one for human beings?'

Similarly in 1985 the Church of England, appalled at the condition of our inner cities and the national policies that seemed to leave them disadvantaged, issued a famous report entitled *Faith in the City*, setting out the policies Christians wanted to see. It drew immediate caustic response from the then government, but was widely welcomed by others and on the whole has stood the test of time. It is still worthwhile and valid. The Methodist Church has a long tradition of issuing occasional 'Statements' expressing its mind on social issues as diverse as euthanasia and political responsibility, drink and divorce, Sunday observance and the treatment of animals.

Such statements cannot be expected to be binding on all members; they express an approximation to a common mind and are for guidance rather than obedience. Some of them impinge immediately on church discipline – thus if a church were to hold that all divorce is wrong then it would have to refuse the marriage liturgy to divorcees. If it held that smoking is wicked then perforce it would have to ban it from all of its premises whatever the law of the land may say. All these statements can quickly become dated, for society, and the form in which moral issues are thrown up, is in a constant rapid flux. Thus a Methodist statement arguing that all gambling is wrong, issued in 1936, had by the mid-1980s to be reconsidered; the original arguments were seen to be unconvincing, and in 1992 a very different conclusion was reached (maybe unknown to the members of the Christmas Fair committee mentioned above).

What To Do?

This is the age of the 'one issue group', a meeting of people around one specific moral social concern exercising every bit of ingenuity in getting that issue widely known and government policies made responsive to it. Thus groups like Amnesty International, Friends of the Earth, the World Wide Fund For Nature, Jubilee 2000, and the Howard League for Penal Reform, flourish and contribute much vitality to the general social awareness today. In many cases Christians can endorse such groups wholeheartedly; their aims should be well known within the church's life. Often such groups have been initiated by the churches – as with Jubilee 2000 or the World Development Movement or the Christian Education Movement or Church Action against Poverty. The church should be fertile ground for such groups and their support. It should also be fertile ground for encouraging people to go into party politics, despite all the moral ambiguities involved.

To sum up, the church should try to be a community of concerned and lively discussion, and supremely one of healthy worship. Within her life the Bible should be handled responsibly and the official statements treated with interest and respect. She should encourage politics and pressure groups. What about that ardent preacher with which this chapter began? Does he or she represent something else which the churches should be offering to the nation – the prophetic? Undoubtedly. When prophecy has faded from a Christian community it becomes stodgy, complacent, dull. When prophecy flourishes one never quite knows what sharp challenge will arise next, what new shafts of insight will appear, what clarion call from God will erupt amongst us.

But there is a difference between the genuine prophet and the Great Moaner. The latter can only see sin and wickedness and decay everywhere. The prophet – someone uniquely aware of the lively Word of God – sees both decline and promise, both old decay and new life on offer. Prophecy is never merely negative, judgmental, denunciatory. It always shouts God's

What Use Should the Church Be?

'NO' to what is corrupt, but also God's 'YES' to what is creative, often in a surprising manner, opening our eyes to something we should have sensed but hadn't.

Yes, the church should be good soil for prophets, and should always be able to tell the difference between them and the loud moaners. Prophets inspire us to a new grasp on God's will, and for that will to have a new grasp upon us; we can never have too many of them.

Questions for discussion

1. Would it be legitimate for a church to be encouraging its members to join one specific political party?
2. To what extent have we found official church statements on moral issues to be helpful? How can they become better known?
3. How should preachers help to form the moral life of the church?
4. What prophets has the church produced recently? Why do you cite those individuals?

20

How Special Is the Christian Way?

There is usually very little difference between the behaviour of Christians and that of others with a warm human concern. If one went to a local meeting of an Amnesty Group, or Friends of the Earth, or the Community Association, the Christian presence wouldn't be immediately noticeable. Everyone there would be talking about the issues from similar perspectives, and the keenest people wouldn't necessarily be churchgoers. The bond between the participants would be concern for the common good, and the differences of opinion would rarely fall along religious or philosophical lines. This would seem to imply that Christian morality is not distinctive.

The same would be true of meetings of anti-abortionists or nuclear disarmers. Christians, particularly Roman Catholics, have been fervently against abortion, but so have many others. Some Christians, especially from the 'peace churches', have firmly opposed nuclear warfare, but so have others. Christians have no monopoly of concern about any of these highly important issues. Meanwhile, in the immediate neighbourhood, the concern of some Christians for those in need will be very noticeable – but so will be that of many other kind-hearted folk. It is quite understandable that critics of the Christian position will often say that 'One doesn't have to go to church to do good.' That is absolutely right. One doesn't.

Thus for Christians to claim that their morals are 'better' than anyone else's would smack of ignorance and bigotry. Time and again Christian leaders and Emperors have proved to be as appalling as those of other faiths. And outstanding saints have appeared from the ranks of every religion – for every Mother Teresa a Mahatma Ghandi – and Christians, of all people, should rejoice that this is so.

Recently, however, Christian morals have come in for sharp attack from some humanists, who argue that Christians are encouraged to be infantile (obeying slavishly a God who issues umpteen orders to his people), to be self-seeking (doing good in order to get finally to heaven), to be conceited (thinking that only their system is really good) and to be prone to bigotry (hence the rise of fundamentalism). Humanists, who aim to concentrate solely on the well-being of others, reckon that their 'faith' (which is faith in human beings) is superior on all counts. This attack makes it clear that, at least in the eyes of these critics, Christian morality is not simply different from their own, but worse by far.

The problem with arguments about which morality is better or worse is the standard by which one is judging, Is there some universally-agreed method by which different moral systems can be assessed? No, there isn't. It is pointless, therefore, to make claims about which morality is 'better' or 'worse'. What we can do is to enquire into the particular quality and character of the Christian ethic, without attempting any comparison or the special pleading that usually goes with it.

The Christian ethic has its origins in the fact that God makes a personal claim upon us. He, the God who is Father, Son and Holy Spirit, calls for our trust and our obedience to his will. That is the heart of the matter. Our ethic is part of our response to God, our trying to show our allegiance to him, our attempt to say, 'Nothing else really matters, except what you desire of me.' Our experience is that everything about us, our deepest needs and longings, are somehow put profoundly right when we have committed ourselves in that way.

A friend recently went into a Russian Orthodox church for the first time, and was fascinated by the furnishings and arrangement of the little building. But the overwhelming memory was of the icons – those exquisite and somewhat stylized paintings, mostly of Jesus, which seemed to be everywhere. He counted fifty-seven of them! Afterwards he commented on the powerful reminder they were to him about his faith. 'I realized with sudden force, all over again, that I

What To Do?

must look to him all the time,' he remarked. Quite so. Christians believe that God's will was made plain and was earthed in the life and death and resurrection of Jesus. Our allegiance means that we see in Jesus the supreme teacher, exemplar, icon of what Christian living should be.

Matthew's mother was saying this when she referred to Jesus as the Ideal Man or 'Ideal Person', the one who was 'totally open to God'. Christian hymns rehearse it again and again:

> Jesus, my Truth, my Way,
>   My sure, unerring Light,
> On Thee my feeble steps I stay,
>   Which thou wilt lead aright.
>
> My Wisdom and my Guide,
>   My Counsellor, thou art;
> O never let me leave thy side,
>   Or from thy paths depart!

Thus Jesus is a focus of all that God wants from us, a constant inspiration and encouragement and challenge. But in almost every Christian church Jesus is not merely indicated by a picture (for, on the whole, Christians know that pictures are inadequate) but by a Cross or a Crucifix. Thus there is nothing ethereal, abstract, remote or sentimental about these reminders of Jesus. Instead they speak of the real, harsh, sin-ridden world in which goodness is repudiated and love can become a fatal sacrifice. Jesus is an unusually damaged hero figure, bearing terrible burdens, yet finally vindicated.

And now a further stage. This being so, the Christian ethic inevitably finds its main source of guidance and refreshment in the New Testament. This is the record of those who knew Jesus and shared his ministry, and those who soon afterwards became his followers. Since Jesus is a focus for Christian worship, guidance, direction and vision, then inevitably the reflections of those nearest to him in human history are crucial. The New Testament is not an infallible record, nor is it understandable without the Old Testament which paved the way for it, but it is the indispensable record, the one to which the early church gave its imprimatur.

Finally, the Christian ethic is special in that it is constantly invigorated by the livingness of Jesus amongst his people, for which the appropriate theological term is the 'Holy Spirit'. In particular, this is manifest in the constant forgiveness of Jesus by which the Christian believes he or she is pardoned day by day and, with confidence renewed, helped to face the future again. Christians marvel at such generosity in their devotions and rehearse it over and over again in their worship. For all is 'of grace'.

So there is good ground for saying that the Christian ethic is different, special. It is a response to the worldview which sees God as the source of all that is, the truth behind all truths, the origin of all life and all value. 'God' is in many ways the term Christians use to describe what others call 'reality'. But God is the source of all personhood, and of the call to each of us to be fully and wholly persons. The nature of a full-blooded response to that call is seen in Jesus, whose significance is spelled out in the New Testament and celebrated in the church's worship.

Some scholars argue that this introduced some very distinctive features which the ancient Romano-Greek world found astonishing. It meant that Christians were unusual in that time for upholding humility as a virtue. Nobody else did. And many Christians taught that agape-love was the pre-eminent virtue. Nobody else did. Those two features are essential in the moral systems of all Christians today, but it is inappropriate, as we have seen, to pronounce the Christian way superior to others, especially since Christians have not been outstandingly humble and loving throughout recent history. The most that can be claimed is that these virtues are integral to the worldview

What To Do?

which Christian faith promotes, and that they therefore help to make it distinctive.

Questions for discussion

1. What differences have you noticed between the morals of Christians and those of other people?

2. Can you suggest standards, not specifically Christian, by which all moral systems could fairly be judged?

3. What is there about Jesus' moral teaching or example which is unique?

4. Which other well-known hymns vividly rehearse the nature of the Christian moral life?

21

Jesus and Compromise

In 1886 a remarkable young French aristocrat, Charles de Foucauld, was converted. He had been a soldier, a playboy, an explorer – all with immense determination. Now he decided, with even more energy, to become a Christian. He was intense, totally dedicated, and desperate to master himself and abandon all to Christ. Soon he became a monk, and in 1897 felt that he must follow in the footsteps of Jesus, haunt the places Jesus had known, be poor and despised like Jesus. So he went to live in a shack outside a convent in Nazareth. In 1900 he became a priest, but a highly original one. He lived as though he would die that day as a martyr. Then in 1905 he went to live in the wild deserts of Morocco, where no other Christian had ever managed to survive. He was murdered by a Tuareg in 1916, but out of his work and writing sprang an extraordinary movement – the Brothers and Sisters of Jesus, now spread worldwide in the service of the poor.

Was Charles plainly absurd to try and live exactly like Jesus? After all, he had no family in Nazareth, no trade to follow there, no chance to go on a preaching mission round Galilee declaring original insights into the purposes of God and offering healing power. In the last resort, as Charles found out, we can't actually reproduce everything about Jesus in our own lives. Nor, as Matthew's mother remarked, should we be so silly as to presume that Jesus knew what it is like to be married, to have three children and to work for the National Health Service. Jesus isn't, then, an example for us to try to follow. He wasn't a prototypical figure for his followers to copy exactly. Nor was he a first explorer into new territory, with every later traveller walking carefully in his footsteps.

Jesus was the *exemplar of the life truly open to God*, the ideal instance of all the virtues perfectly realized in a recognizably human life. He was the demonstration in practice of the

What To Do?

commands of God being heeded with total obedience. He was someone who was so vividly aware of the authority of God over his life that he too could speak and behave with an authority which took everyone's breath away.

It follows that, in the Christian life, we aren't commanded by God to keep in mind a long list of the great virtues – like love, compassion, justice, courage, endurance, humility and so on – but to look to Jesus as the one who sublimely lived out God's will. We aren't commanded to speak as Jesus did (which would involve learning Aramaic), to have the same family life as he did (which would mean being single), to do the same work (which would mean being a carpenter-builder and then a preacher), or to live in the same place as he did (which would cause considerable overcrowding in Nazareth). We are commanded to see in his life the glory of God coming across to everyone who really wants to see it. As we saw above, Jesus is an 'icon' for us, a special sign of God revealed in human flesh.

It isn't surprising, then, that Jesus hardly ever said to anyone 'Do exactly as I do.' Instead he was always saying, in effect, 'See things as I see them. See and hear God as I see and hear God. Love God as I do. Love others as I do. But don't go in for slavish imitation.' To be accurate, there was one instance when Jesus is reported to have said, 'I have given you an example, that you should do as I have done to you' (John 13.15). The verse refers to the time when Jesus, meeting for the last time to share supper with his disciples, washed their feet before they sat down. Clearly, however, Christians don't understand the saying literally – we don't, after all, start every church meeting with someone washing everyone else's feet – but rather as an example of the sort of attitude we should have towards each other. That is, we don't see this act as the sort of 'example' that must be slavishly followed but as a vivid picture of how we should relate helpfully to each other.

In similar vein the New Testament writers don't exhort us to be copies of Jesus, but to 'live in Christ' or to 'have the mind that was in Christ' or to 'put on the life of the Spirit', or some such phrase. They are saying that the Christian ideal, focussed on Jesus – the 'Ideal Person', as Matthew's mother put it – is fully expressed by him. They are saying that our weakness and folly and sin have been embraced by Jesus and killed so that the liberation and exhilaration of a new, resurrected life can also be passed to us by him. They are saying, in short, that Jesus is also the one who conveys to us the forgiveness, guidance and strength to lead the new moral life. Jesus is 'Lord', to whom we may well address our prayers. This is a far more profound discovery than that of simply seeing Jesus as a splendid moral teacher who told some fascinating parables, but died a somewhat unfortunate death. Christian experience is that Jesus is very much more than a fine teacher. For he is the One who grasps our lives for God, bears the pain of our sins, cleanses us from our past and starts us on the new way. That is, to use the technical term, he is 'Saviour'.

Thus an early Christian writer, probably not Paul but someone greatly influenced by him, can say, 'If you have been raised with Christ, seek the things that are above ... for you have died and your life is hid with Christ ... put to death therefore what is earthly in you ... and put on the new nature ... but Christ is all, and in all' (Colossians 3.1, 3, 5, 10, 11). If we find all this rather exaggerated and too idealized for comfort, we can reflect that it was addressed to ordinary people who were having a very hard time trying to live the Christian life and, as the New Testament makes clear, were often making a quite dreadful mess of it. To these people, who were very much like us, the writer was saying, 'Because you are constantly being given, quite dramatically, a fresh start, you can think boldly and in remarkable new ways about the moral life.'

So in the Christian life we don't try to be replicas of Jesus but we can't think too highly of him. Jesus is infectiously inspiring. We can't get away from him nor do we want to. He seems to be

What To Do?

always there – a picture of the good life, a stimulus to it, and an encourager in it. Nor is Jesus an unrealistic figure. Indeed, one complaint often brought is that he is always seen as the 'man of sorrows' who died on the cross, and that this is morbid. Some extreme devotion even suggests that God came amongst us in Jesus solely to die and scar the earth with his blood. But though God's coming in Jesus was a truly earthy business, with rejection and danger, horrible suffering and cruel death, it ended in vindication and new life. The fullness of Christian devotion, therefore, must contain all these elements. For those who genuinely desire to live for Christ, suffering is well-nigh inevitable in this sort of world – but so is renewal.

Nevertheless Jesus' teaching and the frank impossibility every Christian finds in trying to follow it can't be ignored. As the young mother saw very clearly, if her children turned the other cheek every time they were hit in the playground, they would end up being hopelessly bullied. The police sergeant, moreover, seemed to think that talk of turning the other cheek could be relevant for life in heaven, but not for handling villains here below. Do we then make constant compromises, adapting Jesus' noble commands to mundane situations? Of course we do, sometimes knowingly but often unwittingly. In particular, the 'Sermon on the Mount' (Matthew 5–7), which is a unique collection of much of Jesus' moral teaching, has prompted intense discussion throughout Christian history. Here, for example, are three of the ways Christians have thought about the impossible challenge of these chapters:

1. Christians can be divided into two groups: one group follow Jesus' teaching in its totality by becoming 'religious' (i.e. going into a separated community, such as a monastery or convent); the others live in the ordinary world and do their best, but don't expect to reach perfection by total obedience. There are two major problems with this viewpoint. Jesus never talked as if he was addressing only some of his followers; and in

cloistered communities people have actually found it as hard to obey Jesus as in the outside world. (Monks may not often strike each other but selfish and cruel thoughts are as besetting in a monastery as anywhere!)

2. The Christian lives in two kingdoms all the time: the kingdom of Christ and the kingdom of the World. In the former, the commands of Christ can stand a chance of being obeyed; in the latter, they can't. In the former, God's rule is expressed through the gospel; in the latter, the sword is in constant use, as one restrains evil forcefully and keeps order by using all the powers of the State, its police and its magistrates. There are great snags with this view too. For Jesus never talked of two kingdoms in which our behaviour must be radically different, or of a kingdom of this world in which force held sway. For him life was all of a piece in one kingdom.

3. Jesus' teaching and his call for perfection applies to that blessed state when the End has happened and Christ's rule on earth has come about. But there is a major difficulty here too: for Jesus never seemed to view the situation like this; and in the Sermon on the Mount he talks plainly of a very sinful world indeed, in which people hit you and persecute you and think ill of you – a world that is nothing like heaven!

None of these three attempts to reconcile the overwhelming demands of Jesus to the practicalities of everyday living are very convincing. Most Christians adopt a different strategy. They see Jesus' ethical goals as always to be aimed at, yet always beyond us, The fact that we settle for something less must always shame us but never depress us; and we must always keep before us the vision which Jesus offers – fresh, inspiring and encouraging. One moralist, frankly accepting how paradoxical this seems, taught famously that we should see Jesus calling us to the 'impossible possibility'; and many have stressed that we must work for justice between peoples, because that is the corporate expression of love in an imperfect world.

What To Do?

If one criticizes these Christians for making compromises, they inevitably reply that they have no alternative. In an imperfect, unfair and often vicious world, one has to make such compromises or else sink. No businessman can lend to others, expecting nothing in return, as the Sermon on the Mount requires. No policeman – and no child in the playground – can turn the other cheek. No magistrate can be endlessly forgiving. Nobody with family duties can simply give things away whenever asked. There are, then, necessary compromises which every Christian makes every day.

There is, however, another kind of compromise – the kind which stems from moral weakness – which rightly earns moral disapproval. If I have promised to help my brother financially at the year end, but then, because a friend comes and pleads her own need, I decide to give to her instead, I have gone back on my promise. I have shown that I don't keep my word. If in business I accept a bribe from someone, but it is dressed up as a 'gift', then I have compromised the standards rightly expected of businessmen. If a policeman winks his eye at an offence done by a friend, then he is compromised in the way he has handled his authority. These are culpable examples of moral weakness, arising from forgetting Jesus altogether, whereas the others – examples of moral necessity – aren't especially blameworthy, since the people involved are wrestling with Jesus' commands.

Questions for discussion

1. A famous description of Jesus was 'the man for others'. How adequate do you find that? Are other descriptions more satisfactory?

Jesus and Compromise

2. In this chapter Jesus' teaching was summed up as 'See things as I do.' Is that satisfactory? How would you sum up the gist of his teaching?

3. Do you find some devotion to Jesus frankly morbid? In what ways can we ensure that it is more wholesome?

4. How do you attempt to justify the fact that none of us obeys the strong commands in the Sermon on the Mount?

5. What sorts of compromise do you find deplorable? Why?

22

So Where Have We Got?

In following Matthew on his many interviews and meetings and reflecting on the issues raised, several things become abundantly clear:

- One can easily be misled by the Bible, for it contains some moral teaching/commandments/judgments which Christians, living in the light of Christ, find grossly abhorrent.
- The Bible doesn't describe one standard way of discovering God's will for us in the moral life. Many types of ethics lie alongside each other, and many methods are used to determine our moral obligations.
- The Bible offers us unique insights into the way God deals with humanity, shows us where to learn about the character of God, and gives us definitive news about Jesus Christ. This is what makes it indispensable.
- For our moral guidance Jesus is neither example nor prototype nor pioneer; he is an exemplar, an icon, the Ideal Person. A hymn called him 'Way, Truth, Light, Wisdom, Guide, Counsellor'. The aim of the Christian, as so much of the New Testament puts it, is to have the mind that was in Christ.
- This inevitably means that, in this fallen world, we have to adapt the teaching of Jesus to the sinful realities of life, to make basic compromises. But these must be compromises of faith, not of moral weakness.
- The Christian is helped to make ethical judgments by four factors – the Bible witness, the traditions of the church, the experiences of Christians, and the use of reason. The Bible isn't to be regarded as an authority on its own.

After that there are many other observations to be made:

So Where Have We Got?

- Individuals have moral systems to live by and professional codes by which to operate – and many of them are enlightened and helpful.
- Moral relativism, by contrast, is wholly insecure; it trivializes morality.
- Christian morality is not necessarily 'better' than that of others – but it is distinctive, for it is focussed on Christ and assumes a distinctive worldview.
- The command to love is an inadequate basis for a truly Christian morality, in which there is a place for rules and the teaching of the church.

Now let us try to earth all this by an illustration from ordinary experience. Consider the following instance of faithful Christian people trying to cope with a difficult moral dilemma. Greg and Marjorie are in their late thirties and have two children, aged one and three. Greg is an insurance manager, and he and Marjorie planned their family at a time when, since he had a fairly good job, they thought she could give up working as a secretary and devote six years or so to the young children. But suddenly Greg's firm was bought out and he was offered a lesser job at a lower salary. There was little he could do but accept it, but as a result they had to draw on their savings and, when they ran out, found themselves in financial trouble. Marjorie rang up her old firm to enquire about job prospects. Her former boss was delighted, called her for interview and offered her a job as his p.a. She noticed that the place had gone decidedly up-market. He stressed that the firm was booming and explained that she would have to put in forty hours a week, but be available for other extra times and on occasion go for two to three days to Brussels, with extra pay. As part of a dynamic go-ahead team, she would need to be well dressed and ready to act as hostess to important meetings. Normally she would take home at least £240 p.w., but often the extra duties could bump it up to £400 or more. Marjorie was

What To Do?

bowled over, and said she would give her answer next week. 'And sometimes,' added the manager, 'we have to work over the weekend. Double pay, of course.'

She rang a friend, who said that there was a job going at her school for an assistant secretary. 'Just the job for you,' she said. It was for three days a week and nothing in the holidays. During the term she would bring home about £140 p.w., but there was a good chance that it would soon become full-time because the secretary was about to retire. Marjorie was much attracted to it. But then another friend, who ran the local bookshop, spotted her there and asked if she would act as assistant manager for her. It meant working every morning and all day on Saturdays and taking home just over £100 p.w. But there was a possibility of taking over as manager in the near future. Marjorie was delighted with the way so many opportunities were opening up, but she and Greg were worried stiff about what to do. When they went to church on Sunday their anxiety was obvious, and all their closest friends talked with them.

Some said that Marjorie should go for the good salary – but she and Greg wondered what that would do to family life, with the children being looked after by child-minders all day, at considerable expense. Some said, 'Money is never the most important thing.' And Marjorie was not sure about the slick world of the business, and the extreme demands it might make on her. 'These firms don't care two hoots about your family. They want you to treat them as a god,' said somebody. Somebody else told her to find an answer in the Bible. Others said that God would give her some sort of 'hunch' or 'sign' if she asked, but she and Greg replied that they did not favour that sort of idea. Someone said, 'Do the most loving thing for your children.' A young woman said to Marjorie, 'You must go for the job that offers you the most personal fulfilment,' but she and Greg felt that there was more to it than that. Several people said, 'Pray about it; it will be made plain,' but they both replied that that was they had been doing, and it had not as yet been made plain at all. When Marjorie rang her parents, who were living sixty miles away and needing as much support as she could give them, they said, 'It's up to you. We hope you will always pop over to see us every week if you possibly can.' She felt awful then, and again when an old uncle said, 'Just ask what Jesus would do.'

They rang the minister and spent much of Sunday afternoon with him. He told them to sort out their priorities, and helped them with it. Financial security came near the top, involving about £150 p.w., but not as high as the children's welfare and the strong bonding the two of them had already forged with them. Marjorie's happiness and fulfilment came somewhere next, and her parents' welfare soon after. Then Marjorie added her dislike of the 'fast modern world' and her fear that it could make her a different person, a person she didn't really want to be, and that it would make it harder for her 'to be a Christian'. The minister gently reminded her that the bookshop was selling some very dubious stuff now that there was a large student clientele using it.

Finally he said, 'Try to brood on these priorities and to have the mind that is in Christ.' Then he said that the ball was firmly in their court, prayed with them, and that was that. Just as they were leaving Greg turned to him and asked, 'When we make a decision, can we ever be sure we are absolutely right?' The minister paused and said quietly, 'No, we can't – at least, not immediately. We live by faith, not sight; we have to manage with a reasonable assurance, not certainty. Sorry, that's how it is.' Greg replied, 'Thank you for that. It is one of the most comforting things anybody has said to us this weekend.'

What To Do?

Questions for discussion

1. Do you wish to add any further observations to those listed above?
2. How helpful is it when someone suggests that you 'ask what Jesus would do'?
3. Have you any other suggestions about how Greg and Marjorie can be helped in this decision-making process?
4. Are Christians right to fear the 'fast modern world'? Why? What should we do about it?
5. Was the minister's final remark, that we can find no absolute certainty, fair? In what ways can this be comforting?

Further Reading

Peter Vardy and Paul Grosch, *The Puzzle of Ethics*, Collins, Fount 1994, ISBN 0-00-627701-2.

This is a very readable introduction to the history of ethical thinking and to the major contemporary issues; it is not confined to Christian thought only.

Richard G. Jones, *Groundwork of Christian Ethics*, Epworth Press 1987, ISBN 0-7162-0399-5.

This is an introduction to Christian ethics and the ways Christians are responding to the major issues of our time.

David Atkinson, *Pastoral Ethics*, Lynx 1994, ISBN 0-7459-2850-1.

This concentrates on specific issues of our time, using several experts in the more specialized fields and covering a wide range. It is well produced but devotes little space to moral theory.

John Barton, *Ethics and the Old Testament*, SCM Press 1998, ISBN 0-334-02718-7.

This is a brief, clear introduction to the subject by a prominent Old Testament scholar

Leslie Houlden, *Ethics and the New Testament*, Pelican 1973, ISBN 0-14-021573-5, reprinted T&T Clark 1992, ISBN 0-567-29217-7.

A scholarly work, which assumes a knowledge of biblical study and its methods and is packed with information presented in clear and brief compass.

What To Do?

Keith Ward, *The Battle for the Soul*, Hodder & Stoughton 1985, ISBN 0-340-37278-8.

This is a careful analysis of the moral teaching behind many widely-accepted modern viewpoints and techniques. It offers a vigorous critique of them, plus a strong defence of the Christian moral tradition.

Kevin Kelly, *New Directions in Moral Theology*, Chapman 1992, ISBN 0-225-66639-1.

Shows how sensitive Roman Catholic moral thinking can be in the hands of one of its best exponents. It is very well written.

The Common Good, Catholic Bishops Conference 1996, ISBN 0-949005-86-X.

A lucid account of Roman Catholic social teaching, drawing on the tradition developed over the last 120 years and relating it to modern British society.

www.ingramcontent.com/pod-product-compliance
Lightning Source LLC
Chambersburg PA
CBHW070926160426
43193CB00011B/1585